Of Hackeborn Mechthild

Select Revelations of S. Mechtild, virgin

Taken from the Five Books of her Spiritual Grace

Of Hackeborn Mechthild

Select Revelations of S. Mechtild, virgin
Taken from the Five Books of her Spiritual Grace

ISBN/EAN: 9783337428242

Printed in Europe, USA, Canada, Australia, Japan

Cover: Foto ©Lupo / pixelio.de

More available books at **www.hansebooks.com**

Mediæval Library of Mystical and Ascetical Works.

SELECT

Revelations of S. Mechtild,

VIRGIN,

TAKEN FROM THE

Five Books of her Spiritual Grace,

AND

TRANSLATED FROM THE LATIN

BY

A SECULAR PRIEST,

Author of "The Book of the Visions and Instructions of B. Angela of Foligno," "The Life of V. Grignon de Montfort," etc., etc.

Trahe me post te, in odorem curremus unguentorum tuorum; oleum effusum nomen tuum.

Our Lady of the Sacred Heart, pray for us.

London:
THOMAS RICHARDSON AND SONS,
26, PATERNOSTER ROW; AND DERBY.
1875.

CONTENTS.

Book I.

PAGE

Prologue 1
Of the childhood, zeal, and sufferings of Mechtild, the virgin 5

CHAPTER
I.—The Annunciation of the B. Virgin Mary ... 9
II.—Of the twofold Voice of our Lord 13
III.—Of Christ's most sweet Nativity 14
IV.—How she prayed for the Congregation ... 17
V.—Of the Purification of the Most Blessed Virgin Mary, and of Anne, her mother 20
VI.—Of the Mountain with Seven Steps. — Of the Throne of God, and of the Most Blessed Virgin Mary 25
VII.—Of the Name of our Lord, and of His Wounds ... 33
VIII.—Of the Tree of the Cross 35
IX.—Of the Passion of Christ 38
X.—The Passion of Christ, continued 44
XI.—A Hymn of praise and prayer on the Joys of Christ our Lord 53
XII.—How God the Father received His Son at His Ascension 56
XIII.—Of the threefold operation of the Holy Ghost in the Apostles and in every soul 62
XIV.—Of the venerable Assumption of the most glorious Virgin Mary 65
XV.—How the most Blessed Virgin was assumed ... 68
XVI.—Of the Angels, and how men are made their companions 72
XVII.—On the Feast of All Hallows 76

CHAPTER	PAGE
XVIII.—Of the least of the Saints, and God's goodness ...	84
XIX.—How our Lord should be praised in His Saints ...	86
XX.—Of the Feast of Dedication	89
XXI.—Of the Most Blessed Virgin, and of the seven servants who followed her	93
XXII.—How a man may obtain true holiness ...	96
XXIII.—Of the Joys of the glorious Virgin Mary ...	100
XXIV.—Of the Ave Maria	102
XXV.—Of the Ave Maria to be said before Communion	104
XXVI.—Of the Fidelity of the Blessed Virgin Mary to her Son	106
XXVII.—How the Blessed Mary may be saluted ...	107
XXVIII.—Of the Salutation of the Blessed Mary ...	112
XXIX.—How the Virgin Mary asked that three Ave Marias should be said daily	114

Book II.

I.—How God inviteth the Soul	116
II.—Of our Lord's vineyard, which is the Church, and of four kinds of prayer	119
III.—Of our Lord's Scourge	124
IV.—How our Lord gave her Love to be her Mother ...	125
V.—How she was made one with her Beloved ...	127
VI.—How God adorneth the Soul with holy virtues ...	131
VII.—How our Lord's Heart was seen under the similitude of a lamp	136
VIII.—Of the Cross and our Lord's silken vestment ...	142
IX.—Of her threefold pain	144
X.—How she gave all the Saints to drink of the Well of Mercy	147
XI.—How she was called by God together with Love, and of the psaltery of ten chords	149
XII.—Of the Title and usefulness of this Book	152

Book III.

CHAPTER	PAGE
I.—Of the Ring set with seven stones	154
II.—Of the Rose which went forth out of the Heart of God	158
III.—That God ought to be praised in three ways	160
IV.—How man should salute the Heart of God	163
V.—How a man should live in accordance with God's good pleasure	165
VI.—How man should salute the Heart of God	167
VII.—What man should do to atone for his negligences, and how our Lord cometh in seven ways at the Mass	171
VIII.—How man may drive away sloth	175
IX.—Of the threefold unguent of love	177
X.—How man should recommend his faith to God	180
XI.—Of the five sighs, with which man should go to sleep	181
XII.—Of the Wedding-garment	183
XIII.—In what the soul may be made like unto God	184
XIV.—That God desireth our heart	185
XV.—What is the highest good that man can do	188

Book IV.

I.—How men may best advance in the religious life	190
II.—What best preserves a man in the religious life	192
III.—Of three things acceptable to God	193
IV.—That those who are still alive are most happy	194
V.—What man should do when he is in sadness	196
VI.—How man should commit all his grievances to God	197
VII.—That whatever the Soul desireth should be sought in the Heart of God	199
VIII.—How Christ supplieth the defects of a man out of His own fulness	200
IX.—In what way man ought to have recourse to God	202
X.—Of the three ways	204

CHAPTER	PAGE
XI.—That God is ready to receive those that are penitent	205
XII.—A letter sent by Mechtild to a certain Matron	207
XIII.—A letter to a Matron, who was her spiritual daughter	211

Book V.

I.—Of the Charity of B. Mechtild to the dead	214
II.—Of a Sister who was sick	215
III.—Of the soul of an Infant	217
IV.—How, and with what intention, the Lord's Prayer should be said for the departed	218
V.—That we can be purged from venial sins by works of charity, but our mortal sins must be blotted out by the Sacrament of Penance	224
VI.—How we ought to pray for those who are captive in body or in soul	226
VII.—How God commended this His handmaid to His own Mother	227
VIII.—Of the praiseworthy conversation of Blessed Mechtild	228

Revelations of S. Mechtild,
VIRGIN,

Taken from the First Book of her Spiritual Grace.

PROLOGUE.

THE graciousness and humanity of God our Saviour, Who was manifested so mercifully unto the human race by His Incarnation, shining forth day by day more and more, are still through His condescension abundantly shown forth even to us, and in us, upon whom the ends of the world have fallen. Therefore, how many marvels God hath worked in His elect, no word of man can explain; how many gifts He hath poured forth upon the soul that loveth Him faithfully, no tongue can tell; how graciously and with what honeyed sweetness He showeth Himself unto her, she alone meriteth happily to experience.

But in a special manner, how many gifts He hath poured forth on a certain soul that hath loved Him with her whole heart, it is now our desire to relate, so far as our littleness prevaileth, by the help of God.

Now these innumerable heavenly secrets she looked at indeed with the eyes of the soul, but by reason of the littleness, for which she thought herself very vile, she would not tell, save only so far as those who were familiar with her compelled her; and even those things which she told, partly she subtracted from, partly to God's praise, although hardly compelled even by obedience, she told. These things then, which we learnt from her own narration, we will now write according to our measure, in the name of Jesus, to the glory of the Most High and Worshipful Trinity. Wherefore, most dearly beloved, we beg in Christ of every one who shall read this little book, to give thanks to our

Lord for all the grace and good that have flowed forth upon this soul, or at any time upon any soul, from Him Who is the well-spring of all good things. If however he find anything set down with not enough of clearness or of literary skill, this in charity let him pardon as to those who have no experience in writing, because as Blessed Augustine saith, it is the nature of a good disposition to love the truth in words, and not the words themselves.

Although the whole of this book may be said to be about revelations and visions, and although almost in each lesson profit and instruction may be found, yet in order that those who read it may find more easily what thing they look for, it is divided into five parts. In the first of these are placed the revelations concerning the feasts throughout the year, and about certain Saints, and especially about the Most Blessed Virgin Mary. In the second part will be found certain facts in relation to the person to whom these things have been shown; and in these the readers and hearers will find no small devotion, whilst they will be stirred up to love. In the third part are inserted instructions, relating both to God's praise, as well as to man's salvation. In the fourth are placed instructions almost similar, which are both useful and comforting to men; whilst the fifth concerneth the souls of the faithful departed, how, namely, they have been seen and helped by her. All, therefore, on whom God hath poured out the spirit of His charity, that charity, I mean, "which believeth all things, hopeth all things, beareth all things," and those also who aspire to the grace of God, let them all receive this book of spiritual grace with a devout mind, in order that they too may merit to obtain all the good things that are written therein and promised by God. If however any one shall find therein aught that cannot be proved by Scripture, although it be not opposed to the Gospel and the Scripture of God, let him commit it to God's grace, Who now, as of old, manifesteth, when He willeth, to them that love Him, the uncertain and hidden things of His Wisdom and Goodness. We beg also of all who shall read this book, or hear it read, to offer some little praise to Christ for the same happy person, or at least to be grateful for this, that now that the world is growing old, and men are sunk in inveterate torpor with respect to every good, God still deigneth by such incitements to renew both it and them.

OF THE CHILDHOOD, ZEAL, AND SUFFERINGS OF MECHTILD, THE VIRGIN.

THERE was a certain virgin so prevented from her infancy with blessings, that when as soon as born she seemed to be already about to breathe away her spirit, they brought her in haste to be baptised by a priest, a holy and just man, who was on the point of celebrating Mass. And when he had baptised her, he prophesied, as is piously believed, and said: "Why fear ye? The maiden shall by no means die, but will be a Saint and a religious, and God will work many miracles in her, and will consummate the days of her life in a good old age." Now that her baptism was hastened, arose from this, as Christ Himself afterwards revealed to her, namely, that without delay her soul might be dedicated as a temple unto God, and that His grace might wholly dwell in her, and possess her from her mother's womb.

Moreover, when she was seven years old, it came to pass on a certain day, that her mother, together with the little child, went to a cloister not very far from where her parents were then staying. And here, against her mother's will, she remained with exceeding joy, and asking of her own accord the sisters one by one to take her into their company, she obtained her request, nor afterwards could her parents remove her either by threats or blandishments.

Then straightway in a marvellous manner did she begin to grow fervent in God's love and in devotion, and her spirit frequently to rejoice in God with exceeding sweetness. Progressing therefore from day to day, she reached the height of all virtue. She was a maiden of marvellous sweetness, of great humility, of much patience, a lover of poverty, and of exceeding great fervour and devotion, making progress above all in charity, with regard both to God and man, she showed herself loving and serviceable unto all. Wonderfully too was she moved with the zeal of affection towards those who were in trouble and temptation, and like a true mother did she minister unto them comfort and help in all things, so that whosoever went to her returned consoled and instructed. By all was she loved exceedingly, and every one sought her company, so that from this she seemed to suffer many hindrances. But in the midst of this God began to become familiar with her, even while as yet she was very young.

Lastly, in such profusion had God poured out all things upon her, not only in spiritual and gratuitous, but also in natural graces; that is to say, in science and understanding, and in rich gifts of voice, that in all things was she held to be most useful in the cloister, just as if in her our Lord had forgotten none of His good things. Moreover our gracious Lord so continually held His scourge over her, that almost constantly she suffered from pain of the head, and disease of the hair, and exceeding heat of the liver. And all these things most gladly and willingly she bore, counting this alone a pain like that of hell, that ever more and more she desired to enjoy the honeyed sweetness of the grace of God, and to be consoled thereby according to the desire of her heart, and yet was unable, according to her strength, earnestly and fully to cleave to her Beloved, in that happy union by which the soul is made one spirit with God.

Chapter I.

The Annunciation of the B. Virgin Mary.

ONCE when the Gospel "*Missus est Angelus Gabriel*" was being read, she saw the Archangel Gabriel, the guardian of the most Blessed Mary, the Virgin, coming into Nazareth, and holding in his hands a royal standard, on which were written letters of gold. He was followed by an innumerable multitude of angels, who arranged themselves round the house in which the glorious Virgin lived, forming, as it were, a wall from earth to heaven, and in such a manner that within the Angels were the Archangels, and within those the Virtues, and then the rest of the Angelic orders, so that each order surrounded her house like a wall. Then came our Lord, like a Bridegroom from His chamber, beautiful above the sons of men, together with the fiery choir of the Seraphim, who are nearest to

God. These surrounded our Lord and the Most Blessed Virgin after the manner of a wall and a roof. Now our Lord stood near the Archangel's standard, like unto a Bridegroom most delicate and young, and waited until the Angel Gabriel had reverently saluted the illustrious Virgin. Moreover, as soon as the Blessed Virgin had plunged herself into an abyss of humility, and had said, " Behold the handmaid of the Lord, be it done unto me according to Thy word;" straightway the Holy Ghost, with the expanded wings of divine sweetness, entered into the Virgin's soul, and happily brooding over her, and making her fruitful of the Son of God, He caused her both to become in a marvellous manner a mother of a noble burden, and at the same time a Virgin untouched. Thus was the Virgin made the Mother of God and of men, by the witness of the Holy Ghost.

Now when the time was drawing nigh for that most noble banquet, in which our holy maiden was to receive the Beloved of her soul, even Jesus, in the Communion of His Most Sacred Body and Blood, she heard Him say to her: "Thou in Me, and I in thee, and I will not leave thee for ever." She however did nothing else but try to praise God with all her heart. Then our Lord gave to her His divine Heart in the likeness of a golden cup, marvellously decorated, and He said: " By means of My divine Heart thou shalt always praise Me; go now and offer the living chalice of My Heart to all the Saints, that they may be happily inebriated thereby." Then went she to the Angels and offered to them that chalice of salvation, but they did not drink, although they were refreshed thereby. Next she went to the Patriarchs and Prophets, and offered it to them, saying: "Receive Him whom ye have desired, and so long looked for, and make me to long after Him with all my might, and to sigh after Him night and day." After this, she went to the Apostles, and said: "Receive Him Whom you have so ardently loved with your whole heart, and make me fervently to love Him above all things, in the very marrow of my heart." Then turning to the martyrs she said: "Behold Him for Whose love ye have shed your blood, and delivered your bodies unto death; obtain for me that I may spend all my strength in His service." Moreover, going to the Confessors she said: "Receive Him for Whom ye have left all things, and have despised the delights of the world, and make me for the love of Him to despise the things of earth, and to mount up to the summit of true religion." Hastening then to the Virgins, she said: "Receive Him to Whom ye have vowed your virginity, and make me to persevere in chastity of mind and body." And amongst them she saw a virgin who had lately died, and whom she knew well, for on earth she had been familiar with her, and she asked her if things were as she had told her, while she was yet alive. And she answered and said: "Of a truth all things are so: only I have found a hundred fold."

After this she returned to our Lord, when she had made the circuit of the heavenly place; and He took that cup, and placed it in the heart of her soul, and thus was she happily united with God.

CHAPTER II.

Of the twofold Voice of our Lord.

ON the Sunday *Populus Sion* while they were singing: *Auditam faciet Dominus gloriam sociis suis*, she desired to know what was the voice of the glory of the Lord. And our Lord said: "This is the voice of My glory, when the soul, penitent rather from love than from fear, grieveth for her sins, she meriteth to hear from Me these words: 'Thy sins are forgiven thee; go and sin no more.' For straightway that a man hath perfect contrition for the things that he hath done, truly and fully do I forgive him all his sins, and take him into My grace, as if he had never sinned. Secondly, the voice of My glory is when the soul, united with Me by intimate prayer or contemplation, heareth Me say: 'Come, My beloved, show Me thy face.' Thirdly, the soul, when about to go forth out of the body, is thus sweetly invited by Me to her rest: 'Come, My chosen one, and I will place in thee My throne, for the King hath desired thy beauty.' Fourthly, on the day of judgment, this will be the voice of My glory, when I shall summon all whom I have chosen from everlasting, and called to the kingdom of beauty and of glory, and shall say: 'Come, ye blessed of My Father, receive the kingdom which hath been prepared for you from the beginning of the world.'"

Chapter III.

Of Christ's most sweet Nativity.

ON the most sacred night of the sweet Nativity of Christ it seemed unto her as if she were on a rocky mountain, on which was seated the Blessed Virgin, who was near her delivery. And when the time of her delivery was at hand, the Blessed Virgin was filled with unutterable joy and jubilee, and the light of God shone round about her, so that with amazement she quickly rose, and falling down in her boundless humility to give thanks to God, she bowed herself to the earth, not knowing how it went with her, until she held on her bosom Him Who is the fairest of the sons of men. Then with unutterable joy and most fervent love she took the Child, and imprinted upon it three most sweet kisses, by which she was as closely united with the most Blessed Trinity, as was possible for any one to be united with God, without personal union.

By this mountain is figured the spiritual habit, which seemeth hard and rough in this world, and which Christ and His Mother were the first to show and to deliver unto men as an example of true religion. Moreover, it seemed unto her, that her soul sat near the Blessed Virgin, and desired with a great desire to kiss also the lovely Little One. Now the Virgin Mother, after that she had sweetly embraced and addressed her Son, gave Him also to her soul to be embraced by her. Then with unutterable love did she take the Boy, and pressed Him to her heart, and saluted Him with these words, which never before had she thought of: "Hail, marrow of Thy Father's Heart, sweetest meat and most blessed refreshment of the soul that languisheth, I offer unto Thee the marrow of my heart and soul for everlasting praise and glory." For she understood by the inspiration of God, how the Son is the marrow of His Father's Heart; and as marrow is comforting and healthful and sweet, so hath God the Father given unto us His Son, Who is Himself health and the sweetness of all sweetness, to be our defender and Saviour, and most sweet comforter. Moreover the marrow of the soul is that exceeding great sweetness, which she meriteth to receive from God alone, and to feel by the infusion of love; and this truly despiseth all things, and with it, all the joys of the world, even if they were to be infused into one man, cannot be compared.

From the face also of the Boy, there beamed forth four rays, which filled the four quarters of the world, by which were signified Christ's most holy conversation and doctrine, which have enlightened the whole world.

CHAPTER IV.

How she prayed for the Congregation.

ON the holy night of our Lord's Circumcision, as she was offering to God the prayers of the sisters and the homage of her devotion, and as she was praying Him to confer upon them the blessing of the new year, our Lord answered her, and said:

"Health and benediction be unto you from My Father, and from Me, Jesus, His Son, and from the Holy Ghost, Who is the sanctification of all your works. I am He of Whom it is written: '*Thy years shall not fail.*' Come over to Me, all ye who desire Me, and learn of Me that I am meek and humble of heart, for every one who desireth to find rest of heart and body, must needs be meek and humble." And He added: "He who wisheth to renew his life, let him do as a bride doth, whose great love it is to receive from her bridegroom little new year's gifts. So, too, let the soul desire to be clothed by Me in new vestments, so that during the whole course of the year, she may go forth in glory, like a queen, before the eyes of all.

"First, then, let her desire to receive from Me a purple garment, that is humility, so that in the same humility in which I came from heaven to earth, in all things she may bow herself humbly down to everything that is vile. Next let her seek for a vestment of scarlet, that is patience, that patiently she may embrace all that is grievous and hard, because for this did I take My Humanity, that I might suffer pains and reproach. Over these let her be clothed with a vesture of gold, that is, with charity, that in the same love in which on earth I showed Myself affable and kind to all, she may present herself before all men, friendly and gracious. Moreover, when the year hath run its course, let her ask for this to be renewed afresh, and more and more let her exercise herself in these virtues; and, as it were anew, let her strive to keep them.

Now, while she was praying, that whatever in these things was displeasing unto Him, might be circumcised, our Lord made answer and said: "Be ye circumcised in heart from all thoughts of pride, impatience, and worldly vanity. Be ye circumcised in your mouth from all words of detraction, vain complacency, and rash judgment. Be ye circumcised also in deed from sloth, from lukewarmness in good, and from the transgression of God's commandments, and from disobedience."

By our Lord's words she understood that it is a great crime when a man judgeth his neighbour. And if it happeneth that he judgeth him unjustly, he will be as guilty as if he had done the evil which he judgeth. But, if a man hath done that which is said of him, and he who judgeth, knowing not the intention of him who hath done it, formeth his judgment according to his own heart and intention, then, by that very judgment, he becometh as guilty as the man who did that thing; and, unless he wash it away by penance, he will lie under the same penalty as the other.

Chapter V.

Of the Purification of the Most Blessed Virgin Mary, and of Anne, her mother.

ON the holy night of the Purification of the most Blessed Virgin Mary, she saw the glorious Virgin Mother herself, carrying in her arms the Royal Child Jesus, clothed in a vesture of blue, like the blue of heaven, covered with flowers of gold; and on His Breast, and round His neck and arms was written that Name which is sweeter than honey, the Name of Jesus.

And she said unto her: "O sweetest Virgin, didst thou so adorn thy Son, when thou didst present Him in the temple?" And our Lady said: "Not so, yet even from the birthday of that same Son of mine, did I delightfully prepare Him, and with joy beyond all thought did I sigh after that day, on which I was to offer my Son to God the Father, as a most acceptable oblation, by which every oblation that hath been offered from the beginning of the world hath been made acceptable to God. And with such great devotion and gratitude did I offer Him, that if the devotion of all the saints were transfused into one man, yet could it not be compared with my devotion. But all my joy was turned for me into bitterness at Simeon's words: '*Thine own soul a sword shall pierce.*'"

Many times also, when I cherished my Son upon my breast, for the exceeding great sweetness of my devotion, I leant my head upon His Head, and shed so many tears, that I watered His Head and His whole Face with the tears of my love. Very often, too, I said to Him this word: "O health and joy of my soul!" Moreover, while she gazed with panting desire upon the Boy, the Royal Mother, according as she wished, laid the Boy upon her breast, and she was filled with joy. Yet, when she wished to embrace Him, she embraced herself, but did not touch the Boy.

Then, when they began the Antiphon: *Hæc est quæ nescivit thorum in delicto*, she heard the choirs of angels singing in the air with sweet harmony: "*Hæc est quæ nescivit.*" And through the whole Psalm *Benedixisti* did those blessed and angelic orders sing in the air for jubilee in alternate choirs, the Antiphon, "*Angels, Archangels, Thrones and Dominations, Principalities, Powers, Virtues.*" But when they came to the names of those fiery choirs, the *Cherubim and Seraphim*, so sweetly did they sing, that no sound of earth could be compared with it.

Then the most Blessed Virgin stood in the middle of the choir, and held up her Boy in her arms, and there appeared a glory three cubits high above the earth, which surpassed a thousand suns in brightness, and upon which the Virgin Mother placed her most sweet Son. By the glory is signified the Godhead, because God was the Bearer of Himself on earth, and the Godhead ruled the manhood. Now the glorious Virgin had upon her head the Royal Diadem, which two angels held over her head, and on this the merits and dignities of all the saints were enamelled, as it were, with gold and precious stones; of all those saints, namely, who had served her in this life with devoutness of heart. And there hung from it jewel-droplets, by which was expressed the grace which God pours forth upon all those who devoutly serve His Virgin Mother in this life.

There also walked before our Lady the Archangel Gabriel, carrying in his hand a sceptre of gold, on which was inscribed in golden letters, *Ave Maria, gratia plena, Dominus tecum;* and by this she knew that he is honoured with a special dignity in heaven, in that he merited above others to salute so marvellously the Mother of God.

Then the Blessed Virgin stood at the right of her Son, having in her hand a pyx of gold; and when she asked of her what she had therein, our Lady answered: "It is the Blood of the Heart of God, which I wish to offer to my Son, together with all the toil which I have undergone in His service."

Near to the altar she saw Simeon standing, and from his heart there went forth a threefold glory, in shape like a rainbow. By this she understood the humble, strong and fervent desire which he had for God. And she said unto him: "Ah! obtain for me a true desire to be dissolved and to be with Christ." And to her, Simeon said: "Better and more perfect is it for thee to do God's Will, and to wish what He wisheth."

Then she besought the Blessed Virgin to pray for her, and for the congregation, to her Son, which straightway our Lady did on bended knees.

Chapter VI.

Of the Mountain with Seven Steps.—Of the Throne of God, and of the Most Blessed Virgin Mary.

ON the Sunday *Esto mihi*, she heard the Beloved of her soul, Jesus, speaking to her in a sweet whisper of love : " Wilt thou dwell with Me for these forty days and nights?" And the soul said: "O, how willingly, Lord Jesus; this is what I wish; this is what I desire."

Then He showed unto her a mountain exceeding high, and of marvellous greatness, stretching from the East even unto the West, having steps by which ascent was made unto seven fountains. And taking her, He came to the first step, which was called the step of humility, and on it was a fountain that washeth the soul from all the vices that pride hath committed. After this they mounted up the second step, which was called that of meekness, and on it was a fountain that washeth the soul from the stains which anger hath wrought. Next they mounted the third step, which was called the step of love, and on it was the fountain of charity, in which the soul is washed from all the sins which she hath committed through envy and hatred. On this step God stopped awhile with the soul. Then the soul fell down at the feet of Jesus, and straightway that most sweet organ, the mellifluous voice of Christ, sounded in her ears, and said : " Arise, My beloved, and show Me thy face." And the whole company of angels and saints who were on the mountain, so sweetly sang together the bridal-song of love with God and in God, and so modulated was the psalmody, that no words of man can describe it.

Then they mounted up the fourth step, which was called the step of obedience. Moreover, there was a fountain thereon that cleansed the soul from all that had been done through disobedience. After this they came to the fifth step, which was called the step of self-restraint, and in it was the fountain of liberality, that purgeth the soul from all that had been committed through avarice, in that she had not made use of creatures both for her own service and for God's praise, as she ought to have done. And soon they ascended the sixth step, which was called the step of chastity, and there was the fountain of divine purity, that purifieth the soul from all the desires of the flesh, which have made her fall. And there she saw our Lord and others clothed in white garments. Afterwards they arrived at the seventh step of true magnanimity, in which the fountain was called spiritual heavenly joy, that cleanseth the soul from all sins of sloth. Moreover, this fountain flowed, not with force like the others; but little by little, and drop by drop, it welled forth, because no man can take his fill of heavenly joy, as long as he is in this life, for it is only, as it were, a drop in comparison with what it is in its reality.

After this the Beloved, with His beloved, went up to the mountain top, where there was a multitude of angels in the likeness of birds, having golden bells, and giving forth sweet sounds. On the mountain itself were two thrones that shone with marvellous splendour.

The first was the throne and seat of the Most High and Undivided Trinity, from which there went forth four rivers of living waters. By the first river she understood was signified the Wisdom of God, by which He governeth the saints, so that they recognize His will in all things, and cheerfully fulfil it. By the second river is figured the Providence of God, by which He provideth all good things for them, and richly satisfieth them with interior bounty and liberality. By the third are shadowed forth the riches of God, with which He inebriateth them with the plenty of good things, so that never do they desire anything so great, that it is not even more abundantly poured out upon them. By the fourth river is typified the Will of God, in which they live so pleasantly in God, satiated with the fulness of joys, abounding in delights, of which there is no end, and where God wipeth away all tears from the eyes of the saints. The first throne was surmounted by a finial of gold, of such great magnitude, that it filled the earth, and by this was signified the Godhead, and it was gemmed with precious stones, and by reason of its pure gold it shone forth as the royal canopy of the King of Heaven. It had also many tabernacles, the habitations, namely, of the holy patriarchs, and prophets, and apostles, and martyrs, and confessors, and all the elect. But the second throne was that of the Virgin Mother, who, as becometh the Queen, deservedly sat by her King. And this throne, too, had many tabernacles, those, namely, of the virgins who had walked in her footsteps, the holy virgins who worthily follow after the Virgin Mother.

Seeing, then, Jesus the King of Glory on the throne of His imperial magnificence, and His Mother on His right hand, for wonder at that most gladsome face on which the angels desire to look, she fainted away within herself altogether, and fell down before the throne of the Holy Trinity at the feet of Jesus. Then our Lord raised her up, and laid her sweetly on His Heart. Now, her garments were a little sprinkled with dust about the borders, by reason of something which had occupied her thoughts at vespers, and the Blessed Virgin came and wiped it away.

Thereby she prayed the most Blessed Virgin to praise her Son for her. And straightway our Lady went from her throne together with the choir of virgins, and extolled Him with praise unutterable. The patriarchs also, and the prophets, praised our Lord with jubilee, saying: "To the Most High Trinity, One God, be one Godhead, equal glory, co-eternal Majesty, to the Father, and to the Son, and to the Holy Spirit, Who subjecteth the whole world to His laws." Moreover, the glorious choir of the apostles sang with exulting joy: "From Whom are all things, by Whom are all things, in Whom are all things, to Him be glory for ever;" for Him they had known on earth, from Whom all good things flow, and by Whom all things have been made in heaven and on earth, and in Whom all good things are hidden.

After this the victorious army of martyrs sang, and said: "To Thee be honour." Then the order of confessors sang their hymn: "Benediction, and glory, and wisdom, and thanksgiving, honour and virtue, and power be unto our God for ever and ever." And amongst them she saw especially her glorious father, the Blessed Benedict, and he was clothed in a white garment, interwoven with colours like those of the rose. By the whiteness was figured his virginal chastity, and by the rose colour was signified that he was truly a martyr, because with such great labours he had poured forth his sweat in the rigour of his order, and gloriously had triumphed over all.

And when she marvelled that the angels did not sing, our Lord answered: "Thou shalt sing with the angels." And straightway the angels sang together with that blessed soul, and said: "All the angels praise Thee, O holy Lord, in the highest;

praise and honour become Thee, O Lord!" After this she besought our Lord, saying: "O only Love, in what doth it please Thee most to be known by men?" And our Lord said to her: "In the goodness, with which I mercifully wait for man, until he be turned to penance. Thereupon, immediately, I draw him to Me by My grace. But when in no wise he willeth to be converted, then, justice requiring it, he must needs be damned." She also asked of God to instruct her, how she might make satisfaction for the members of the Church, who, at this time, were heaping so many insults on His own beloved Son. And our Lord answered: "Read Me three hundred and fifty times the Antiphon: 'To Thee be praise, to Thee be glory, to Thee be thanksgiving for ever and ever,' for all the insults that are so unduly heaped upon Me by My members."

Chapter VII.

Of the Name of our Lord, and of His Wounds.

DURING the Mass, *Nos autem gloriari oportet*, our Lord said to her: "Attend to these words: *in quo est salus*. In the Cross is true salvation, and out of it no salvation is found. In whatsoever soul, therefore, there is not the Cross, that is, tribulation, there is no patience; and where there is no patience, there is no salvation. In the Cross, also, true life was given to man, when I, Who am Life Itself, and Who died upon the Cross by the death of love, have quickened the soul that is dead in sins, and given it again to live eternally in Me. By the Cross, too, is it given to a man, as often as he falleth through sin, so often to rise again through penance, and, moreover, there is given to him the resurrection of the flesh, and eternal liberty."

And when they were reading the Epistle, *Dedit illi nomen quod est super omne nomen,* she said to our Lord: " My Lord, which is the sweetest Name that hath been given Thee by Thy Father?" And our Lord said to her: " That Name is, *The Saviour of all ages.* For I am the Saviour and Redeemer of all that is, and that hath been, and that shall be hereafter; I am the Saviour of all who lived before I became Man; I am the Saviour of those who lived in the time when I, as Man, conversed with men; I am the Saviour of those who have followed My teaching, and who still wish to walk in My footsteps, even unto the end of the ages. This is that most worthy Name, which was pre-ordained for Me alone by the Father from the beginning of the world, and this Name is above every name."

Moreover, when her soul gave thanks to God for His most holy wounds, and prayed Him to inflict upon her as many wounds of love as He bore in His own Body, our Lord said unto her: " As often as a man groaneth for love at the remembrance of My Passion, so often doth he gently touch My Wounds, as it were, with a rose of spring, and there leapeth forth a dart of love into the soul of that man, by which he is wounded for his health."

CHAPTER VIII.

Of the Tree of the Cross.

LIKEWISE, during a certain Mass, *Nos autem oportet gloriari,* she saw in the middle of the church an exceeding fair tree, that, by its height and widely-spreading branches, filled the whole earth. Now the tree had grown up out of three branches which had sprung together from the earth, and the points of the branches thereof were bent back upon the earth. Under one of the branches were the beasts that fed of the fruit which fell from the tree; and these typified sinners and men who lived like the brutes; those, namely, who enjoy the good things of God without gratitude, like brute beasts, never looking up in thanksgiving to Him, from Whom all good things come.

Under another branch were men who eat of the fruit of the tree itself, and by these were signified whosoever are just in the Church. On the third were birds which sang exceeding sweetly, and by these were made known the souls of the saints, who sing praises to God without end. The souls, also, of purgatory, came under the likeness of cattle, and were refreshed by the sweet odour of the tree. Now certain birds of a black colour flew round about it, but a thick smoke went forth therefrom, and forced them to fly farther away. By the birds of a black colour she understood that the demons were figured, and all the annoyances of men, which a man shall overcome in no better way than by the memory of our Lord's Passion; and this was signified by the thickness of the smoke.

There was a priest, also, who celebrated Mass, and he was vested and adorned with the leaves of the same tree, and little branches full of fruit hung round about him; by which was shown forth, that everyone who loveth and worshippeth Christ's Passion, acquireth the nobler virtues thereof, and whatever good he doeth, turneth more fruitfully to his merit. The hearts, also, of the faithful, were fastened and hung upon the branches of the tree after the similitude of burning lamps, and the oil which burned in those lamps flowed from the tree; by which was pointed out that no man can love God, unless this gift be poured out upon him by the grace of God. Moreover, by this that they were burning, was typified, that every man who wisheth to love God, should recall himself to the thought of His Passion, very often making remembrance thereof, and reflecting thereon, for therein will he have matter enough for love, and there is nothing which so assisteth the mind, and maketh it to burn, as the remembrance of the Passion of Christ.

Chapter IX.

Of the Passion of Christ.

ON the Parasceve, (Good Friday,) while thinking of the innumerable good things which God had done for her, she said unto Him: "O my most sweet God, in what can a man make restitution unto Thee, in that, on this day, Thou didst deign to be taken and bound for men's salvation?" He answered: "If a man of his own free will, and cheerfully, be bound for My sake with the chain of true obedience."

And the soul said: "What praise shall he give Thee, for that Thou wert spat upon with the unclean spittle of the Jews, and beaten with cruel buffets?" Our Lord said to her: "I tell thee of a truth, that all who despise their prelates spit on My Face; if a man desire to make amends to Me for this affront, he ought to love his prelates."

And the soul said: "What thanksgiving shall he make Thee, O most kind One, for the blows which Thou receivedst?" He answered: "By keeping faithfully and strictly to the customs and statutes of his order and religion."

And the soul said: "What praise, O most faithful Friend, shall he give Thee for the pain which Thou didst suffer, when the crown of thorns was pressed down upon Thine Imperial Head, so that that delightful Face of Thine, on which the angels desire to look, was all veiled with rosy blood?" He answered: "By a man's making strong resistance with all his might when he is tempted; and as many temptations as he overcometh in My Name, so many precious gems doth he set on My diadem."

And the soul said: "What shall he give Thee, O wisest of masters, for that Thou wert mocked at as a fool, clothed in a white garment?" He answered: "By a man's seeking nothing ornamental, nor precious in his clothes, but only what is necessary."

And the soul said: "What thanksgiving shall he make, for that Thou, O only Friend of my heart, wert so inhumanly and cruelly beaten?" He answered: "By persevering with Me for the sake of holy fidelity and patience, as well in prosperity as in adversity."

And the soul said: "What, O most loving One, wilt Thou receive in return for having been fastened to the Cross by Thy Feet?" He answered: "That a man should pour back into Me all his desires, and if, together with Me, he cannot have desire, yet let him have the will to possess this desire, and then, of a truth, I receive his will."

And the soul said: "What wilt Thou receive in return for having been fastened to the Cross by Thy Hands?" He answered: "That he should exercise himself in all good works, and avoid all evil works for My sake."

And the soul said: "What, O only Sweetness, ought to be offered to Thee in thanksgiving for that Wound of love, which Thou didst receive on the Cross for man, when unconquerable love, the very arrow of love, pierced Thy sweet Heart, from which flowed forth Blood and Water for our healing, and when conquered by the mightiness of love, Thy spouse, Thou didst die the death of love?" He answered: "That a man should conform his will to My will, and that My will should always, in all things and over all things, be acceptable unto him."

Our Lord also said unto her: "Of a truth, I tell thee, that if a man shall shed tears out of devotion to My Passion, I will receive them, as if he had suffered for Me."

And the soul said: "Ah! my Lord, by what kind of devotion shall I be able to come unto these tears?" He answered: "I will teach thee. First think, with what friendship and love I went forth to meet My enemies, who sought to put Me to death with swords and staves, as if I had been a robber and a malefactor; but I went forth to meet them as a mother to her child, in order that I might snatch them from the jaws of wolves. Secondly, when they smote Me with cruel buffets, as many blows as they gave Me, so many sweet kisses did I give to the souls of those who, even unto the last day, are to be saved by My Passion. Thirdly, when they most fiercely scourged Me, so efficacious a prayer did I pour forth for them to My Heavenly Father, that many of them were converted. Fourthly, when they pressed the crown of thorns upon My Head, as many thorns as they pressed upon Me, so many gems did I place in their crown. Fifthly, when they fastened Me with nails to the Cross, and stretched out all My Members, so that My bones and inward parts could be numbered, with My whole power did I draw towards Me the souls of all who have been predestinated to life eternal, as before I had said: 'When I shall be lifted up from the earth, I will draw all things unto Me.' Sixthly, when they pierced My Side with the lance, out of My Heart I gave drink out of the chalice of life to those who through Adam had drunk of the cup of death, in order that they might all be made the children of eternal life and salvation in Me, Who am Life."

Moreover, when she received the Body of Christ, our Lord said unto her: "Wouldst thou see how I am now in thee and thou in Me?" And she was silent, for she deemed herself unworthy. And straightway she saw our Lord, as it were, a pellucid crystal, and her own soul, as it were, most pure and glittering water, flowing through all the Body of Christ. Then she marvelled much at the unutterable gift of God, and at His wonderful goodness towards her. And our Lord said to her: "Remember what Blessed Paul, My Apostle, writeth: 'I am the least of the apostles, and am not worthy to be called an apostle; but by the grace of God I am what I am. Thus thou, too, art nothing in thyself, but what thou art, thou art by the grace of God in Me."

Moreover, when, according to custom, the Cross was laid in the sepulchre, she said unto our Lord: "Now, O only One of my heart, bury Thyself in me, and bind me inseparably to Thee." He answered:

"I will bury Myself in thee; I wish to be the enjoyment of thy senses, and the exercise of all thy senses and acts."

Chapter X.

The Passion of Christ, continued.

IN like manner, on the holy night of the Parasceve, she said in her prayer unto our Lord: "My most beloved Lord, in what can I recompense Thee for having on this night been taken and bound for me?" He answered: "In desire and good will; for these two things are, as it were, the heavenly cords with which thou shalt sweetly bind Me to thy soul. For a heart that is of good will, and prepared for every good, easily admitteth Me. Moreover, useless thoughts, that come upon it unforeseen, are, as it were, no sin, yet so if, after advertence, the heart dwell not upon them voluntarily and with deliberation." And He added: "When I delivered Myself up into the hands of wicked men, they bound Me, and did upon Me whatever they would, yet they could not bind My tongue; but I, Myself, so bound My tongue, that I would speak no word, save what was useful." Thus ought every man, who hath the power of speaking good or ill, in like manner to bridle his tongue.

Now, about the hour of Prime, as she was meditating how at that hour Christ stood for judgment before the governor, our Lord said unto her: "Come with Me to judgment." And He took her, and set her before His heavenly Father. Then all the saints, together with all creatures, made complaint over her.

The Seraphim accused her of having often, through sloth, extinguished the divine love within herself, by which she had been set on fire by God, or by the Heart of God. The Cherubim cried out against her that she governed not herself according to the light of the knowledge of God, by which she had been enlightened above the rest of women. The Thrones complained that often she had disturbed their most peaceful King, Who had established His throne within her, with useless thoughts. The Dominations said that she had not bowed down with due reverence and trembling, as was fitting, before their King and Lord. The Virtues made complaint, that she had not exercised herself in due manner in holy virtues. The Archangels said that she had not listened, as was meet, to God's sweet talk, nor sent up sweet and loving whispers to her Beloved, by those who were sent unto her as His ministers. The Angels lamented that she made unworthy use of their ministry.

The Blessed Virgin complained that she had been unfaithful to Him Who was both her and God's most sweet Son, and Whom she had brought forth to be a Brother to her. The Apostles cried out together that she had not followed their doctrine with diligent zeal. The Martyrs said that unwillingly had she borne pains and infirmities. The Confessors accused her of having negligently acted in religion, and in her spiritual exercises. The Virgins complained that she had not loved so loving a Lord with her whole heart. All creatures with one voice cried out together, that she had made unworthy use of them.

Then said our gentle Jesus to the Father: "For every complaint that hath been objected against her I will answer, for I confess that I am led captive by her love." And God the Father said unto Him: "What hath compelled Thee to do this thing?" He answered: "My election; for I have chosen her for Myself from everlasting." Then the soul, trusting in the grace of so great an Advocate, confidently took Him in her arms, and said to the Father: "I present to Thee, O worshipful Father, Thy most humble Son, Who hath well paid Thee for whatever I have sinned through anger; I present Thee also Thy most loving Son, Who is the love of Thy Heart, and Who hath fully supplied for whatever I have been guilty of through hatred. His overflowing liberality hath paid whatever I have sinned through avarice; His holy zeal hath made amends for my sloth; His exceeding abstinence hath supplied for all my intemperance. The purity of His most innocent life for everything I have done wrong, whether by evil thoughts, or words, or deeds; His deep obedience, by which He was made obedient even unto death, hath blotted out all my disobedience; His high perfection hath wholly made excuse for all my imperfection."

About the hour of Tierce, she saw our Lord surrounded with a glory and a splendour that cannot be uttered, so that, from the sole of the foot to the crown of His Head, He flowered all over with ornaments of singular beauty; and this He had received in reward for having been so inhumanly scourged for us. He had also upon His Head a garland of divers flowers, exceeding fair, of so marvellous a workmanship, that her soul had never seen the like; this Christ had made for Himself of the divers pains which He suffered in His Head.

About the hour of Sext she saw our Lord carrying His Cross, and all the congregation, together with herself, came to Him, and each one laid her grievances and burdens upon the cross, as if they were green leaves; and all these our Lord most graciously received, and with great patience and joy carried them together with His Cross. Moreover, all the sisters helped our Lord to carry it.

About None our Lord appeared to her in marvellous glory and majesty, and He had on Him a collar of gold, and attached to it was a golden shield containing all kinds of sufferings; and it covered our Lord's whole breast, having on the upper part thereof a most pure lily, and on the lower an exceeding fair rose. By this shield was figured the victorious Passion of Christ; by the lily His innocence; by the rose His exceeding patience. Moreover, when the sisters came up for Holy Communion, our Lord gave to each person His own Divine Heart, filled with excellent spices of marvellous sweetness. The spices also sprang up from every part of His Heart like flourishing and flowering little plants, so that His Heart seemed to be all of flowers. And each one, as she came up, received the aforesaid shield from our Lord, so that the same shield shone with marvellous splendour on each one's breast. And by this was figured that Christ bestowed upon His faithful ones the victory of His own Passion, that it might be for them as a shield and defence against all their enemies.

Moreover, at the hour when she had to kiss the Holy Cross, at the Wound of the Feet, she was inspired by God, and said: "Behold, O my Lord, I fix all my desires in Thee, and I fit them to Thy desires, that henceforth, being fully purified, they may never more be mixed up with the things of earth." At the Wound of the Right Hand, our Lord said unto her: "Here call to mind all thy spiritual duties which thou hast neglected in thy spiritual state, in order that they may be fully restored to thee by means of My own." At the Left Hand, He said: "Here place all thy pains and adversities, so that in union with My sufferings they may be sweetened, and rise up before God as a sweet odour in exceeding patience; even as a garment that hath been laid up in spices exhaleth the same fragrance, or as a crumb of bread dipped in honey taketh unto itself the sweetness of the same." At the Wound of the Heart, He said: "In this Wound of love, which is of such mighty compass that it embraceth the heavens and the earth, and all that in them is, gather up all thy love into My love, that henceforth it may be perfected, and, like an iron glowing with fire, may be brought into one love with Mine."

About Vespers she saw our Lord, as it were, taken down from the Cross, and the Blessed Virgin holding Him on her bosom, and saying to her: "Come and kiss the health-giving Wounds of my most sweet Son, Who for the love of thee underwent death. Imprint three kisses on His Heart, and give thanks to Him for that efflux, by which from everlasting He hath flowed out, and still floweth out, and will endlessly flow out upon thee and all His elect. Kiss the Wound of His Right Hand, for it hath been thy helper and fellow-worker with thee in all thy good works; but kiss also His Left Hand, for in it thou wilt ever find all thy refuge. Moreover, kiss the Wound of His Right Foot, in thanksgiving for the fervent desire with which all the days of His life He ran thirsting after thee. Kiss, too, the Wound of His Left Foot with gratitude, for thou shalt ever find therein the remission of all thy sins. Take, also, three kinds of ointment, whereby thou mayest ceaselessly anoint the Beloved of thy soul: first, the oil of olives, by which is expressed mercy, that is to say, by exercising thyself frequently in works of mercy and kindness; secondly, the oil of myrtles, that joyfully and faithfully thou mayest bear tribulations and infirmities for the love of God; thirdly, the ointment of balsam, so that, taking all the gifts of God with gratitude for His praise alone, thou mayest hope for nothing and desire nothing therefrom, but mayest pour them back upon Him Who is the well-spring and source of all good things."

About Compline the Blessed Virgin came to her, and said: "Take my Son, and bury Him in thy heart." Straightway she saw her heart in the likeness of a silver sarcophagus, and it had a cover of gold. By the silver was signified cleanness of heart, but by the gold the love which keepeth and preserveth God in the soul. When, therefore, she had, as it seemed to her, enclosed Christ in her heart, He said unto her: "Here thou shalt ever find Me in thy heart. And behold I give unto thee a pledge of life everlasting, and to all for whom thou hast prayed to-day."

Chapter XI.

A Hymn of praise and prayer on the Joys of Christ our Lord.

I PRAISE, adore, magnify, glorify and bless Thee, O good Jesus, in that inestimable joy which Thou didst have when Thy most blessed Humanity received glory at the Resurrection from the Father of Divine glory in itself, and imparted the same eternal glory to all His elect in His own Godhead. By this unutterable joy, I ask Thee, O most loving Mediator between God and men, to preserve, by Thy grace, this same glory, which Thou didst then give me, unhurt, that in the day of judgment I may assume it with joy."

I praise, adore, magnify, glorify and bless Thee, O good Jesus, in that unutterable joy, which Thy most holy soul had when it delivered itself up to be the price and the pledge of eternal redemption, both for us and also for that plentiful multitude of souls which followed it out of hell with ineffable rejoicings, and which it presented to God the Father. By that unutterable joy, I ask of Thee, O most loving Mediator between God and men, that at the hour of my death Thou mayest be unto my soul a pledge and a price that may suffice to pay all my debt, and do Thou appease for me God the Father, the most just Judge, and lead me with gladness before His Presence.

I praise, adore, magnify, glorify and bless Thee, O good Jesu, in that unutterable joy, which Thou hadst when there was given Thee from God the Father the plenary power of rewarding, enriching, and honouring, according to the magnificence of Thy bounty, all Thy fellow-soldiers and friends, whom Thou hast freed so gloriously and triumphantly from the power of the tyrant. By that unutterable joy, I ask Thee, O most loving Mediator between God and men, to make me a sharer of all Thy labours and works, and of Thy glorious death and most blessed Passion.

I praise, adore, magnify, glorify and bless Thee, good Jesu, in that unutterable joy, which Thou hadst when God the Father gave Thee all Thy friends for an everlasting possession and inheritance, and when that most gracious petition and will of Thine was fulfilled, in which Thou hadst said: "*I will, that where I am, there also may be My minister,*" so that every joy and every good, which is Thou Thyself, might be theirs without end. By that unutterable joy, I ask of Thee, O most loving Mediator between God and men, to give me that blessed fellowship with all Thine elect, that together with them I may have Thee, my only joy and my every good, for myself and for ever.

Chapter XII.

How God the Father received His Son at His Ascension.

ON the glorious Ascension-day of Christ she saw herself on a certain mountain, and there Love appeared unto her under the likeness of a virgin exceeding fair, clad in a green mantle, and Love said unto her soul: "I am she, whom thou sawest on the holy night of Christ's Nativity, in such marvellous splendour; I am she, who brought upon earth the Son from the bosom of the Father, and now I have exalted Him above the heaven of heavens." And she added: "Fear not, for greater things still shalt thou see." And, of a sudden, her garments were changed into marvellous brightness, and became filled with golden bars, and on each bar there was an image of the King.

And overhead was this inscription: " He who descended, He it is who ascended above all heavens." She understood, also, that all the works of our redemption were, in a marvellous manner, shown forth in those images.

Moreover, our Lord Jesus was clothed in like garments, save that on the bars of His vestment there was an image of Love as of a queen, and thus God was clothed in Himself, because God is Love, and Love is God. Now Love took God in her arms, and lifted Him up on high, and said: "Thou art He alone, in Whom I have fully accomplished all the might of my power."

But the soul asked the virgin what her arms were, in which she had carried God. She answered: " My arms are nothing else but my omnipotence and my will; for I can do all things. But not all things that I can do are expedient, and therefore inscrutable Wisdom ordereth and disposeth all things of mine."

There, too, was seen a great army of saints, amongst whom John the Baptist, and Joseph, the nursing-father of our Lord, and Simeon, who received Christ in the temple, were the primates, and all of these ascended together with our Lord. The most blessed Virgin Mary, the Mother of our Lord, was also seen on the aforesaid mountain, clothed in the same vestments as those of love, and underneath them she wore a tunic of red. And she said to the soul: "All my sufferings which I bore together with my Son, and for my Son's sake, I bore in silence and in patience. I had a ceaseless yearning for the little infant Church before God, and often did I bow myself down before His spiritual mercy, and to the desires of a soul that loveth in such a way He can refuse nothing. Therefore it is, that a soul troubleth God more on earth than in heaven.

Then the soul told the Blessed Virgin of the joy which she felt in the Ascension of her Son. And she was answered: "In that joy, I knew all the joy and blessedness which I was to receive in my Assumption."

Then our Lord Jesus, ascending on high

with jubilee beyond all conception, stood before the Father, and presented to Him in His own Person the souls of all the elect, both of those who were present, and who had ascended with Him, as well as of all those who were to come there hereafter, and the works of each, and the sufferings and the merits; so that they who are now in a state of sin appeared in Him in the form wherein they will be hereafter in heaven. Now the loving souls, and those which bear many things patiently for Christ, shone in His Heart with special splendour; but the rest of the souls shone in the rest of His members.

Then the Father of heaven received His Son with exceeding worthy honour, and said: "Behold, I give Thee the overflowing abundance of delights, which Thou didst, in a manner, leave when Thou didst descend into the exile of the world, together with the plenary power of communicating them in all abundance to all the souls which Thou hast now presented together with Thyself." Moreover our Lord Jesus offered to God the Father all the poverty, disgrace, and pains, all the labour and works of His Humanity, as a new and most acceptable kind of gift never before seen in heaven, although foreseen and foreknown in the Godhead, and all these God the Father so drew into Himself and united them with His Divinity, that it seemed as if He bore them in His own Person. To the Holy Ghost, also, He brought all the fragrance of love, with which His most holy Heart, beyond all reckoning, was burning, and the seven gifts of the Holy Spirit with fullest fruit, for in Christ alone has the Holy Spirit perfectly wrought these gifts, according to that of Isaias: "The Spirit of the Lord shall rest upon Him, the Spirit of wisdom and understanding, the Spirit of counsel and fortitude, the Spirit of knowledge and piety, and He shall be filled with the Spirit of the Lord."

Then He gave to the Angelic spirits the milk of His Humanity, which they had never tasted before, that is to say, a new and overflowing sweetness in His delicious Humanity, for increase of their joy and glory. To the Patriarchs and Prophets He gave to drink of that exceeding sweet chalice, in which He satisfied all their desires, and made them henceforward to rest in Himself. But as for the Innocents, and those who had died for the truth, like John the Baptist, Jeremias, and many others, He, as it were, gilded their sufferings by lighting them up, and ennobling them in His own glorious Passion and Death. Moreover, many gifts did He bestow upon those who were left on earth, upon the Apostles, namely, and the other faithful, for everlasting knowledge of spiritual consolations, and to inflame them with His love.

Then our Lord turned to the soul, and said: "Behold I have ascended triumphant and glorious, and all thy burdens I have taken with Me." And in this word she understood that the necessities and tribulations of all men are present to Him, and that He Himself fighteth gloriously in us and for us, and getteth Himself the victory.

Chapter XIII.

Of the threefold operation of the Holy Ghost in the Apostles and in every soul.

ON the holy Vigil of the glorious feast of Pentecost, as this humble handmaid of God was desiring to show herself a dwelling-place of the Holy Ghost, our Lord said to her: "The Holy Ghost worked three things in the Apostles. First, in that He wholly changed them at His coming, setting them on fire with the love of God, so that they who before had been timid and weak, and lovers of themselves, were made so strong, that they feared not even to die; nay, they thought it a joy and a glory to bear adversity for the love of God. Secondly, even as fire purifieth the iron, and maketh it like itself, so did the Holy Ghost purge the Apostles from all dross, and sanctify them wholly in Himself. Thirdly, even as gold melted by fire, if it be poured into a mould, representeth the form of the mould in itself, so did the Holy Ghost melt the Apostles in the fire of His love, and make them flow into God, and conform them to His image, so that of them that saying of the Psalmist seemed fulfilled: "I have said, ye are gods."

In like manner, let a man who desireth the advent of the Holy Ghost, implore that these three things may be worked in him: namely, that the Holy Ghost may defend him by His love against evil, and strengthen him for every good, by taking away from him all human fear, so that for the love of God he may patiently and gladly suffer adversity. Let him pray through the Holy Ghost, that the remission of all his sins may be given him, and that, wholly melted in the fire of the love of God, he may merit wholly to pass into God, and, happily united with Him, to be conformed to Him.

Likewise the Holy Ghost gave the Apostles to drink out of three chalices, whereby He so abundantly filled them, that not undeservedly the people took them to be drunken. First, with the Wine of love He so abundantly filled them, that, like drunken men, they gave themselves up to oblivion, no longer desiring honour or any bodily convenience, but seeking the glory of God alone.

Secondly, He made them abound with the wine of Divine consolation and sweetness, so that henceforth no earthly joy or comfort could separate them. Thirdly, He inebriated them with the love of heavenly things as with a cup of nectar, and made them, as it were, mad; hence, burning with unutterable desire for our Lord, they even desired, if they could, to go through a thousand deaths.

In like manner let the faithful soul ask of the Holy Ghost to give her to drink in these three ways: the wine, namely, of the love of God, which may bring forth forgetfulness of self, so that she may seek for herself no honour nor convenience except for God's glory. Let her also pray to be so filled with the interior sweetness of the Holy Ghost, that never may earthly joy or delight be strong enough to give her pleasure. Let her pray, too, that she may be inflamed with the love of heavenly and spiritual things, whereby, panting with her whole heart after God, she may look at death and other painful penalties as nothing.

Chapter XIV.

Of the venerable Assumption of the most glorious Virgin Mary.

ON the vigil of the glorious Assumption of the most sweet Virgin Mary, the handmaid of Christ was fixed in prayer, and it seemed unto her as if she were in a little cottage, where, upon a little bed, lay the most blessed Virgin, covered with fair white linen sheets. Then she said to the Blessed Virgin: "Whence is this, O Maiden-Mother, that languor can be in thee, since we believe that thou wert altogether a stranger to the pains of death?"

And she answered: "When I was in prayer, and set on fire with the remembrance of all God's good deeds to me, and with a desire of praising and thanking Him, of which men can have no conception, there came upon me a new fire of the love of God, and stirred up within me an unutterable desire of seeing Him, and of being with Him. When that fire of love had increased so much, that I had no more strength of body, I lay down upon my bed, and all the orders of angels ministered unto me. Then the Seraphim helped my love, kindling in me that divine fire more and more. The Cherubim also ministered unto me the light of knowledge, so that I foresaw in my mind all the great things that the Lord, my Son and my Spouse, was about to do for me; and therefore it was that I said in my prayer, that the spirit of darkness should not come nigh me, lest peradventure his presence might cloud in somewise that heavenly light. The Thrones preserved in me undisturbed the rest which I enjoyed in God. The Dominations stood by me, and served me with the same reverence as that with which princes venerate the queen and mother of their King. The Principalities, by their presence, prevented those who had come to me from venturing either to speak or to do aught that might disturb the quiet of my soul. The Powers drove back the demon-hosts, lest they should dare to approach. The Virtues, for the increase of my honour, stood around me, clad and adorned in my virtues. The Angels and Archangels, by their homage, caused all those who were present to serve me with the greatest devotion and reverence.

And she saw in spirit how the angels flew round about the most glorious Virgin, and the seraphic spirits walked on our Lady's breath. And when she saw the blessed John the Evangelist standing opposite the most Blessed Virgin, she said to him: "By that gift which thou didst offer unto God, when for His Mother's tender love thou desiredst to be deprived of all who were dear to thee, I ask of thee to obtain for me, that I, for Christ's love, may cast away from me all that is dear, so that I may love Him with my whole heart." And he answered her: "So great was the consolation that I drew from the words of my Lord's Mother, that never did I hear from her one word, at which I did not feel special joy."

Chapter XV.

How the most Blessed Virgin was assumed.

ON the holy night of the Assumption, when she was in choir, it seemed to her as if again she were with the Blessed Virgin, who was lying upon her bed. And behold! (as it was given to her to understand,) the height of infinite majesty bowed itself down into the abyss of holiness, that is to say, the most humble heart of the Virgin, and so abundantly filled it with the torrent of its own Divine delight, that her most holy soul, being absorbed, was wholly transfused into God. And thus did Mary's most holy soul go forth from her body with joy unutterable, a stranger to all pain, and flying exceeding gladly into the arms of her Son, and resting with all love and much delight upon His Heart, was borne even unto the throne of the most excellent Trinity, amidst the festal mirth of the Saints. But how God the Father, with the most gracious affection of His whole Fatherhood, then received her soul into His Fatherly Heart, it is impossible for any creature to tell. So, too, was it with the inscrutable Wisdom of God, God the Son; with what exceeding befitting honour He did her filial reverence, and to what a sublime height He stablished her at His Right Hand on the throne of His glory, passeth all thought. Moreover, the Holy Ghost, in His benignity and sweetness, filled her so abundantly with all good things, that all in heaven were filled out of her fulness.

The Seraphic spirits, too, who from the beginning of their creation had burned in the fiery furnace of the Godhead, were yet more inflamed with love by the heat of the Blessed Virgin's charity. The Cherubim, full of the brightness of God, were, in a certain manner, lit up with new light;

and all the orders of angels and of saints obtained greater glory and new joy for the increase of their rewards from the glory of so great a Queen. Then, in the immensity of blessedness, the incomprehensible Trinity flowed in upon her in the fulness of the Godhead, and penetrated her through and through. All full of God, whatever she seemed to do God did in her and by her, so that He saw with her eyes, and heard with her ears, and sung to Himself most sweet and perfect hymns of praise with those virginal lips of hers, and seemed to rejoice and take delight in her virgin-heart, as if in His own.

Now the Queen of glory stood at the Right Hand of her Son, clad in mirror-like vesture, exceeding bright, and in this the good deeds of the Saints shone forth marvellously. Wherefore it was that all the Saints came before her throne with gladness, and contemplated their own deeds, and henceforward they broke out into new praise, and made exceeding sweet jubilee to God. The Patriarchs and Prophets, when they gazed at their own yearnings and magnificent virtues, and the familiarities which they had had on earth with God, discovered that the Blessed Virgin excelled them in all these, because being brighter far than they in grace and virtue, and yearning after God with a closer yearning, she is proved to have been most familiar with God. And so all the orders of the Saints came one by one, and gazed at the works of their own perfection in the Blessed Virgin, as in a mirror, and marvelled in their joy how far she had outstripped them. For amongst the Apostles she was found to have clung the most faithfully to Christ, and most diligently to have kept His words. Amongst the martyrs was she the most patient and constant; amongst the confessors the most enlightened and enlightening by word, as well as by example. Amongst the virgins, not only was she the chastest and the holiest, but she was even the first to cultivate in an eminent degree virginity and the whole religious life. Amongst the meek was she the most meek; amongst the merciful the most merciful; amongst the humble the humblest; amongst the perfect she was the most perfect. Deservedly, therefore, has she gone beyond the excellences of all the Saints. And the most Blessed Virgin said: "Whosoever desireth to be exalted with the highest honour above all men, let him subject himself humbly to all men; and he who would be rich above all men, let him spoil himself wholly of his own will; and he who seeketh after dignity of the highest glory, in all things let him strive to exercise himself in virtues."

Chapter XVI.

Of the Angels, and how men are made their companions.

BEFORE the heart of S. Michael the handmaid of Christ beheld a golden staircase composed of nine steps, with a multitude of angels surrounding it on either side, so that on the first step were the Angels, and on the second the Archangels, and so upwards, in such a way that on each step there was placed an angelic order. And she understood from heaven, that by staircase is signified the conversation of men; so that, namely, whosoever faithfully, and humbly, and devotedly ministereth in the Church of God, and also for God's sake serveth the infirm, or pilgrims, or the poor, and all who, showing love one to another, help each other, shall stand on the first step, and be made equal with the Angels. Those, moreover, who, by prayer and devotion, wait familiarly upon God, shall serve Him on the second step with the Archangels. And they who exercise themselves in patience, obedience, and voluntary poverty and humility, and bravely perform all virtues, mount, together with their virtues, to the third step. Those who struggle with their vices and lusts, and treat with contempt the enemy together with all that he suggesteth, shall obtain a glorious triumph on the fourth step along with the Powers. Those, moreover, who, in the Church, are set over others, and administer well the office committed unto them, and who watch day and night for the gain of souls, these shall possess the glory of the kingdom in return for their labour, on the fifth step along with the Principalities. They, too, who bow themselves down before the divine Majesty with all subjection, and for His glory reverently love every one of their fellow men, nay, even themselves, because they are made in God's image, and who conform themselves to God so far as they can, and bringing their flesh into subjection to their spirit, obtain the mastery over their mind by transferring it to heavenly things, shall exult on the sixth step together with the Dominations. They who diligently wait upon meditation and contemplation, by embracing cleanness of heart and peace of mind, offering unto God a most peaceful dwelling-place, (and these may truly be called the Paradise of God, according to that: "My delights are to be with the children of men;" of whom also it is said: "I will walk in them, and make in them My dwelling-place,") shall be made the companions of the Thrones on the seventh step. They, moreover, who outstrip others in science and knowledge, and who, by a singular blessedness and with illumined minds, look at God face to face, and by doctrine and enlightenment of others pour back upon God all that they draw from Him, Who is the well-spring of all wisdom, shall be placed on the eighth step of the ladder of ascension along with the Cherubim. And they who love God with their whole mind and their whole heart, and who place their whole being in that eternal fire, which is God, and who, being made exceeding like unto Him, love Him no longer with their own, but with His love, even as they themselves are loved, and not only Him, but all things in Him and for Him, and who love their enemies and regard them, and whom nothing can separate from the love of God, nay, nor even hinder, for the more that enemies rise up against them, the more mightily do they grow strong in love,—burning therewith happily in themselves, and setting others on fire, so as, if possible, to make all men perfect in the love of God,—weeping for the vices and sins of others as if they were their own, because it is the glory of God alone and not their own, that they love and search after. These shall come close to God, with nothing between Him and them, on the ninth step, along with the Seraphim, between whom and God no others are found.

Chapter XVII.

On the Feast of All Hallows.

ON the vigil of All Saints, when, from labouring at a certain work which had been enjoined her by obedience, she had neglected to go to Mass, she came at length before the elevation of the most Holy Host, and with sadness of heart offered her negligence to God. And our Lord said to her: "I see not that thou hast with thee so great a ransom, that I can absolve thee from sin?" And she said to Him: "Yes, Lord, I fully trust that Thou canst, and I know that to Thee nothing is impossible." Then our Lord said unto her: "Fully will I answer for thee in all things to God My Father. Do thou also ask the several companies of the Saints to offer for thee their good merits: the Patriarchs and Prophets, the longing which they had for My Incarnation; the Apostles, the fidelity with which they remained with Me in My tribulations, and by going about and preaching gathered together for Me a faithful people; the Martyrs, the patience with which they shed their blood for the love of Me; the Confessors, the holiness by which they pointed out to others, by word and example, the way of life; the Virgins, the chastity and incorruption through which they obtained a place so near to Me."

During Matins she saw the King of glory sitting on a Throne of crystal purity, with burning ornaments of red coral. At His Right Hand sat the Queen on a like throne, but of sapphire, adorned with white pearls. By the crystal throne of God she understood that the inestimable purity of God's worth is signified, and by the coral the rose-red Passion of His Humanity. By the sapphire was figured the heavenly Heart of God's Mother, and by the pearls her virginal purity.

While, therefore, the verse of the second responsory was being sung, namely: *Ora pro populo*, etc., the most glorious Mother, rising from her throne, was seen to kneel down before the King her Son, and devoutly pray for the congregation. In like manner each choir of the Saints seemed to do the same thing, when mention was made of them.

Then, during the eighth lesson, the most Blessed Mary again rose from her throne before her Son, and stood with the marvellous multitude of holy virgins. And behold! from that most sweet Heart of hers, in which lieth hidden the fulness of all beatitude, there seemed to go forth a triple little cord of a golden colour, which, passing through the most loving Heart of the Virgin Mother, was stretched out to each of those virgins' hearts, and so it passed through all their hearts, one by one, until it was bent back from the heart of the last of the virgins, and penetrated through the Heart of God, forming in marvellous shape, as it were, a mystic band. Moreover, the rest of the multitude of either sex, who had not been rendered sublime by the special gift of virginity, seemed to be led about separately from the Virgins, and separately from these, again, the choirs of the holy Angels. And from every heart of the Saints, as well of the Virgins as of the rest of the multitude, there went forth an exceeding sweet musical tone, as of organs. By this it was given unto me to understand, that there was nothing so little that they had done on earth, in thanksgiving, or prayer, or in deed, or in word, or in thought, that will not sound forth from their hearts with sweet sound and trumpet-like through all eternity to God's praise, and to the increase of their own joy and glory. Hence it was brought back to my remembrance that of these it is written: " Then let all the organs of the Saints sound continually," and that other word: "Praise Him with timbrel and choir, praise Him with strings and organs." But by the triple little cord which went out of our Lord's Heart, she understood to be signified the love of the ever adorable Trinity, of the Father, and of the Son, and of the Holy Ghost, which, by the intervention of God's most worthy Mother, hath passed with especial sweetness through the loving hearts of virgins that are incorrupt, and hath united them with God, the Scripture also testifying that Incorruption maketh a man near unto God.

Moreover, during the High Mass, while the Gospel was being read, she sought our Lord, according to her wont, and said: "What, O my sweet and best beloved, wilt Thou have me to do?" He answered: "Yesterday, a certain one told thee." Then she remembered that yesterday she had been forewarned by God, that she should beseech the whole multitude of the Saints to offer for her, and being desirous to obtain this, she heard our Lord saying unto her: "Behold I come at the head of all the Saints to offer for thee to God the Father. And first of all will I offer that most holy time, when I lay resting for nine months in My Virgin Mother's womb, as a bridegroom on his marriage-bed, for that time in which thou didst lie in thy mother's womb, nor yet wert free from the stain of original sin, nor capable of My grace. Next will I offer My most holy Nativity for thy nativity, in which, not as yet washed in the font of baptism, thou wert still an alien to Me. Then, too, will I offer My most innocent infancy and My childhood for the ignorances of thy infancy and childhood, and the fervent zeal of My devout boyhood and youth for the negligence of thy girlhood. After this I will offer the whole course of My holy and perfect conversation together with the fruit and love of My Passion, for all thy faults of commission or omission, so that by Me and in Me all thy defects may be supplied."

Thus, then, after He had said this, the Lord of hosts went forth, and all the host of heaven followed Him, and He went to make His offering at a certain altar, which appeared to be adorned with exceeding wonderful and delightful variety of sculpture, of cunning workmanship. And she understood that there was laid up therein the treasures of the whole, that is, of the Highest and Incomprehensible Godhead, beyond all price and all reckoning. So, too, by the sculpture of the altar, she understood to be signified the inexplicable diversity of the benefits of God, that pass all human understanding. Now there were three steps that went up to the altar aforesaid: and the first of these was of gold; by which was declared that no man can come to God, unless he goeth up to Him by charity. The second seemed to be of the colour of the sky; by which was meant meditation concerning Divine and heavenly things, because he who hath the will to come nigh to God, must needs frequently endeavour to be lifted up from all earthly preoccupations by meditation. The third step seemed to be green; by which was marked the verdant intention of the Divine praise, so that, namely, every operation of ours may be made with such an intention as to desire rather God's praise and glory than our own profit and health. Hence, therefore, about the time of prayer, she saw, also, in the midst of the mystic band, which hath been described above, a pleasant table, laid out exceeding fair, from which our Lord took His deific Body and Blood of the Sacrament of Himself, and gave to the congregation that were seated with Him at the same table. Then, as a munificent monarch, He gave of the Royal feast, by the ministry of the heavenly princes, to each of the congregation. Now the feast, which she saw, she affirmed to be the same as that with regard to which our Lord had taught her a certain devotion before that festival; namely, that, as a sign of special friendship, He would give to each of the congregation a thousand souls, which, in return for their prayers, He would free from the bonds of sin, and translate into the kingdom of heaven.

Chapter XVIII.

Of the least of the Saints, and God's goodness.

ON a certain Saturday, while they were singing the sequence *Mane prima sabbati*, at the verse *Ut fons summæ*, she thought how many and how great were the unutterable good things that had flowed forth, and still ceaselessly flow forth, out of Him Who is the well-spring of all good. And our Lord said to her: "Come and see him who is the least in heaven, and then wilt thou be able to understand the source of goodness."

Now she began to turn over in her mind where she could find such a one, and how she might be able to recognize him. And behold there met her a man clad in a green dress, and his hair was crisp and silvery grey, and he was of moderate stature, exceeding fair in face, and very beautiful.

And she said: "Who art thou?" And

he answered: "On earth I was a robber and a malefactor, and never did I do a good work." And she said: "How hast thou come into this joy?" He answered: "All the evil that I did, I did not out of wickedness, but, as it were, from custom, and because I knew no better, for I was brought up to this by my parents. For this reason, at the last, I obtained God's mercy through penance; and for a hundred years I was in the place of punishment, and underwent many torments; and now, by God's gratuitous goodness alone, I have been brought in here to rest." Then he told the handmaid who saw these things all the good which God so mercifully had accomplished in him. And it was a great joy to her that He could have done this, and thus she recognized the source of goodness in this least one, for if God worked such marvels in him, who had done no good, what will He not accomplish in His just holy ones?

Chapter XIX.

How our Lord should be praised in His Saints.

OUR Lord said: "On the Feast of each Saint thou canst praise Me for the eternal election, by which I elected them. Secondly, for My admirable vocation, by which I called them to the kingdom of glory; for whoever could have access to the Divine Majesty, unless I called and drew him? Thirdly, for the most faithful division of My kingdom with them; for I have established them all kings and queens together with Me, and have made them with such great care, and so gloriously to reign, that they seem to have received, not the half, but the whole of My kingdom."

The Saints also may be reminded of the joy with which they rejoice, because they perfectly know God, and see in their glad delight that they themselves have been

loved from everlasting, and chosen out of
God's free goodness for such felicity. For
no man is able to look into his friend's
heart, and see how that friend is affected
towards him, as My Saints can do, who
search into the interior of My Heart, and
feel with unutterable joy My affection and
love towards them. They can be reminded, secondly, of the exceeding sweet
taste which they enjoy, because, when they
praise and bless Me, and see My love
towards them, it is to them a sweet savour.
Thirdly, they can be reminded, that they
possess the fulness of their own will, because all that they will, that they can most
freely do. So, too, the Saints can be put
in mind of that glorious, splendid, and delicious preparation, which God hath prepared for them from everlasting; namely,
that they may be where He is Himself,
joint-heirs with His Only-Begotten. Nay,
in Himself, in the interior of His own
Heart, hath He given them a mansion.
Secondly, they can be put in mind of that
exceeding sweet influence, by which God
floweth in upon them with the whole of

His divine deliciousness, and they themselves, in sweet fruition, flow back into Him with all their gratitude. Thirdly, they can be told of that most worthy honour, which He hath shown unto them, in that He hath made them to sit at meat with Himself, feeding them and satisfying them without cloyment, with the brightness of His own Face surpassing sweet, and inebriating them with the torrent of the pleasure of God, by fulfilling in good things all their desires. Fourthly, they can be reminded of their most faithful guerdon, because there is nothing so small that they have done for His love, or given up, or borne, which will ever be forgotten, but all things will be diligently kept in mind by Him, and He will reward them above all merit with most worthy honour. Fifthly, they can be put in mind of their eternal beatitude, for they are certain that their glory and felicity will never fail, but, together with the mass of their joys and rewards, will yet ever receive new increase.

Chapter XX.

Of the Feast of Dedication.

ON the Feast of the Dedication of the Church, whilst they were singing at Mass the verse, *Deus, cui adstat chorus angelorum, exaudi preces servorum tuorum*, she saw in spirit the heavenly Jerusalem, and the throne of God therein, which was of such great magnitude, that it extended from the highest heaven down even into hell, and on the lower part thereof was a great bolt, which pressed down all who were in hell; and by this she understood that the justice of God was signified, which most justly separated the wicked from God. Now the city itself was built of precious and living stones, that is, the Saints, so that each Saint, together with all his good deeds, distinctly appeared in the wall, like an image in an exceeding bright mirror. Moreover, all the Angels were drawn up before the throne according to their orders and ranks. And when the soul of the handmaid desired to hear her Beloved, the Angels took her gently amongst them, and led her up to the Archangels, and then the Archangels led her as far as the Virtues, and so she passed through all the angelic choirs, and came even to the throne of her Beloved. And she fell at His feet and said: "I salute Thy most holy Feet, with which, in love and desire that is beyond all reckoning, Thou didst rejoice as a giant to run the course of our redemption and salvation." Then she gave thanks for each good thing which God had done to her. After this she said to our Lord: "What shall I ask now, for to-day we are invited so often to ask, in order that we may find joy also in obtaining our requests?" And our Lord said to her: "Pray first for the remission of all thy sins; for this is very wholesome for a man, and he will obtain therefrom true joy."

Then the soul rose up, and beheld our Lord with outstretched hands sitting upon the throne, and saying: "Even as upon the Cross with outstretched hands I persevered until death, so do I still stand as I stretch out My Hands before My Father for man, and for a sign that I am truly ready to take every man that cometh to Me into My embrace. If, then, a man desire to obtain this, if he be prepared for love of Me to suffer all adversity, it will be a sign that he hath come unto My embrace. Moreover, whosoever shall desire that My ears should reach down to his prayers and grant them, let him be ready for all obedience, for it is impossible that the prayers of obedience should not be received by Me."

Likewise, when they were singing the response: *Benedic Domine domum istam, quam ædificavi nomini tuo,* she saw all the virtues that are named therein, stand before God, in the likeness of virgins, and amongst them was one who excelled all the rest, and she carried a cup of gold, into which each of the virgins placed aromatical spices, and on bended knees before God offered them unto Him. Whilst she marvelled at this, our Lord said to her:

"This is obedience, and for this reason she offereth unto Me alone, for in herself she containeth the good of the rest of the virtues, and the virtue of obedience ought to have these virtues in itself. For he who is truly obedient must have his soul, as it were, sound; that is, must be weakened by no criminal sin. He must also have humility, whereby to subject himself in all things to those who are set over him. Sanctity and chastity must also be in him, because he ought to retain cleanness of heart and body. Strength and victory are needful for him, in order that he may have courage to work well, and to be victorious in resisting vice. The rest of the virtues, also, it is fitting that he should have; namely, faith, without which no man can please God, and charity, both to God and to his neighbour; meekness, which showeth itself gentle and sociable to all; temperance, in order to cut off all superfluities; patience, to conquer all adversities, and to gather fruit of all that is profitless; and spiritual discipline, in order strictly to keep his rule.

And whilst, during all this, she was praying for a certain person, who was burdened by her office, it came to pass that she saw her among these virgins, standing before God, and she heard our Lord say unto her: "Why doth she unwillingly chant to Me, to whom I Myself wish to chant sweetly for everlasting? Moreover, the chant of a single day sung out of obedience, delighteth Me more than all singing that proceedeth from one's own will."

CHAPTER XXI.

Of the Most Blessed Virgin, and of the seven servants who followed her.

ONCE, as she was saluting the most Blessed Virgin in the Mass *Salve Sancta parens*, and asking that she might obtain from our Lord the remission of her sins, it seemed unto her as if the Blessed Virgin stood before God, and she herself was close to our Lady's feet, touching the hem of her garment as it flowed down upon the ground.

And rising up she saw several virgins standing round her, and when she desired to know who they were, the Blessed Virgin said: "All these virgins ministered unto me on earth. The first is Holiness, and she ministered unto me in my mother's womb, by filling me with the fulness of the Holy Ghost. The second is Prudence, and she served me in my childhood, so that nothing childish did I ever do contrary to God's will. The third is Chastity, and she ministered unto me in the Angelic Salutation, when overcome by her love I gave my answer to the Angel. The fourth is Humility, and it was she who made me the Mother of God, whose handmaid I acknowledged myself to be. The fifth is Charity, and it was she who took the Son of God from His Father's Bosom, and laid Him in my womb, and so filled me to overflowing, that even as the hearts of mothers who are great with child are wont to faint away beneath the burden of their pain, so did my heart oftentimes faint away under the burden of its love. And as the hart panteth after the water-springs, so also did I pant after the sight of the Son, whom I bore within me. The sixth virgin is the Zeal which ministered unto me all the works which my Son required to be done to Him, after He was born, so that in Him I accomplished all the Father's will. The seventh virgin is Patience, who ministered unto me from the first hour of my Son's Nativity to the day of His Passion. The Fear of the Lord was my chamberlain, for never did I suffer my feet to slip." Then the soul said: "O Lady, obtain for me these virtues." And she answered: "Go to my Son, and ask Him." Now our Lord was sitting on a golden couch, supported by two columns ornamented, as it were, with sapphire and gold. Then the soul fell at His feet, and prayed for these virtues, that they might be given to her and to all who were tempted. And our Lord assented to her request, assigning to her, as it were, the virgins who stood by, and looking, she saw that each one had in her hand a little lance, and it was sharp.

The sharpness signified the constancy with which vices ought to be resisted; moreover, round about the little lances were placed golden cymbals, which, when they were moved, made an exceeding sweet sound in the ears of God. The cymbals signified the thoughts which a man resists, thus gaining a victory over vice, and by this he maketh melody in God's ears. And she saw, as it were, numberless multitudes of angels and saints standing around. And our Lord said: "All these thousands who here stand by, will be the defenders of all who fight for Me against all the snares of the enemy."

Chapter XXII.

How a man may obtain true holiness.

ON a certain Saturday, while the *Salve Sancta parens* was being sung, the handmaid of our Lord saluted the Blessed Virgin, and besought her to obtain for her true holiness. And our Lady answered:

"If thou desirest true holiness, keep thyself close to my Son, Who is holiness itself, that maketh all things holy." Now as she thought how she might do this, the most gracious Virgin replied: "Keep thyself close to His most holy Infancy, desiring that His most innocent Boyhood may make up for all thy sins of commission or of omission during thy childhood. Keep thyself close to His most fervent youth, which flourished in burning love, so that in Him alone the fire of Divine love had sufficient fuel to make amends for all the lukewarmness and sloth of thy youth. Keep thyself close to His Divine virtues, so that thy virtues may therein be ennobled and exalted. Secondly, keep thyself close to my Son, by directing all thy thoughts, words, and works in Him, so that all the imperfections of thy thoughts, and words, and works may be blotted out by Him, Who never was guilty of any of these things. Thirdly, keep thyself close to Him, even as the bride to the bridegroom, for the bride is fed and clothed out of the bridegroom's goods, and because of his love, loveth and honoureth both his friends and his family. Even so let thy soul be nourished with the word of God as with a most excellent food, and with His riches, that is, by the example of His virtues, which should be imitated so as to cover thee like a vestment and a becoming ornament. To His family, also, that is, to the Saints, keep thyself close, by loving them, and praising God for them, and by very often leading them to thy Beloved, so that they may praise Him together with thee. Thus shalt thou be truly holy, according to that which is written: '*With the holy thou wilt be holy,*' just as a Queen will be a queen from consorting with her King." Moreover when, in the sequence *Ave Maria*, they were singing the words *Salvatoris Christi templum extitisti*, she reminded the Blessed Virgin that she herself was the glorious temple of God, full of light and of delight. Then the Blessed Virgin took her by the hand, and led her to a house exceeding fair, which was built of square stones deeply laid, and which had no window, yet which within was full of light, and the house had a little gate of red and thick jasper, and on it was a little chain of gold. This house typified the glorious Virgin, and the square stones denoted that in the four elements of which man is made up, she was most deep in her contemplation, and full of light in her knowledge. By the gate was signified that unto all who come to her she is as a mother. By its red jasper her marvellous patience was expressed, while the chain of gold typified her love. And the Blessed Virgin said to her: "If thou desirest to become a house of God like unto this, strive to exercise thyself in these virtues." Moreover, the glorious Virgin had in her right hand four rings set with the finest gems, and she placed her right hand on the breast of the soul, and said: "By these gems thou wilt overcome all kinds of temptations. Every temptation taketh its rise from four vices, namely, pride, anger, uncleanness of the flesh, and sloth. If, then, thou art puffed up with pride, oppose to thyself my most devout humility; if thou art troubled with anger, call to mind my gentleness, whereby I was the meekest of all; if thou art annoyed by the uncleanness of the flesh, run and take refuge in my most pure chastity; if thou art tempted by sloth, fly to my burning love, and thus thou wilt beat back the whole power of the enemy."

Chapter XXIII.

Of the Joys of the glorious Virgin Mary.

ONCE, when the glorious Virgin Mary appeared unto her, she asked the Blessed Virgin to deign to instruct her as to what honour she should show unto her on that day. And the Blessed Virgin answered: "Remind me of the joy which I had when the Son of God, going forth like a Bridegroom from the Heart of the Father, came into my womb, *rejoicing as a giant to run his course.* Remind me, in the second place, of the joy which I had when going forth from my virginal womb, He was made to me the Son of sweetness and of joy. Other sons bring to their mothers pain and sorrow; but the Son of God, Who is sweetness itself, brought to me, His Mother, joy and gladness, and was made exceeding sweet. Thirdly, remind me of the joy which I had at the offering of the wise men, in which He was made to me the child of honour, for never was any mother honoured at the birth of her son with gifts such as these. Fourthly, remind me of the joy which I had when I offered my Son in the temple, and when He was made to me the child of cleanness and of holiness, because, even as other mothers are purified in this way, so, too, although I stood in need of no purification, that purification increased my holiness. Fifthly, remind me that in His Passion He was for me the son of sadness and of pain. Sixthly, remind me that in His Resurrection He was made to me the Son of joy and exultation. Seventhly, remind me that in His Ascension He was made to me the Son of majesty and of kingly dignity."

Chapter XXIV.

Of the Ave Maria.

ON a certain Saturday, while the *Salve Sancta parens* was being sung, she said to the Blessed Virgin: "If I could salute thee, O Queen of heaven, with the sweetest salutation that ever the heart of man hath been able to conceive, most gladly would I do so." Then straightway the glorious Virgin appeared to her, having on her breast the Angelic Salutation written in letters of gold, and she said: "Higher than this salutation no man ever yet hath reached, nor can a man salute me more sweetly than he who saluteth me with the reverence wherewith God the Father saluted me by this word *Ave*, confirming by His Omnipotence my immunity from sin, that is, from the guilt either of punishment or of fault. The Son, also, so illuminated me with His Divine Wisdom, that I am the exceeding bright star by which the heaven and the earth are lightened, and this is signified by the name *Maria*, that is, the star of the sea. The Holy Ghost, too, by penetrating me with His Divine sweetness, made me, by His grace, so full of grace, that every man who seeketh grace through me shall find it, and this is signified by the word, *gratia plena*. So, also, at the word, *Dominus tecum*, I am reminded of the unutterable union and operation, which the whole exalted Trinity perfected in me, when It so joined in one person the substance of my flesh to the Divine nature, that God became man. What I felt in that hour of joy and sweetness, no man can fully experience. By the words *Benedicta tu in mulieribus*, every creature recognizeth in wonder, and beareth witness that I am blessed and exalted over every creature, whether in heaven or on earth. By the words *Benedictus fructus ventris tui*, is blessed and extolled that most excellent and superexcellent fruit of my womb, Who hath given life to every creature, and blessed it for evermore."

Chapter XXV.

Of the Ave Maria to be said before Communion.

IT came to pass on a certain day, after Matins, whilst she was in prayer, that she began to doubt whether or not the evening before she had said Compline of our Lady. And being saddened at this, she confessed her negligence to God, and straightway said her Compline. After this she said five *Ave Marias*, according to her wont, before receiving the Body of Christ, the several intentions of which we will here write down for the instruction of others. First, she reminded our Lady of that most holy reception, in which she conceived her Son in virginal purity at the message of an Angel, and in the abyss of her humility drew Him down to herself from His royal throne; and she prayed our Lady to obtain for her a clean conscience and true humility. Secondly, she reminded her of that most sweet reception, in which she received Him, when first she gazed at Him in His Humanity, and recognized Him as very God, praying our Lady to obtain for her true knowledge. Thirdly, she reminded her that at all hours she had been prepared to receive grace, nor ever placed any impediment in its way in herself, praying her to obtain for her a heart always ready for the grace of God. Fourthly, she reminded her of the great devotion and gratitude with which she had been wont on earth to receive the Body of her beloved Son, and had recognized more fully than all others, the greatness of the salvation which accrued to man from this reception, praying our Lady to obtain for her true gratitude. Fifthly, she reminded her of that most loving reception, in which her Son had called her to Himself, praying her to obtain for her grace to go to communion with spiritual joy, because if a man were to realize the greatness of the salvation which cometh to him from Christ's Body, he would faint away in himself for very joy. After this, she felt that the

Blessed Virgin stood before her, and pressed her in a close embrace, but she, beginning to bewail her negligence, asked if the evening before she had said her Compline. And our Lady said to her: "When thou knowest not whether thou hast said it, before my Son it is as if thou hadst not done it."

Chapter XXVI.

Of the Fidelity of the Blessed Virgin Mary to her Son.

ON another occasion, as she was accusing herself before God of having never loved His Mother as she ought to have done, our Lord said to her: "For this thy negligence, praise My Mother for the fidelity with which she served Me most faithfully in all things all her life, ever submitting her own will to My Will in all her actions. Secondly, extol her fidelity, with which she stood by Me most faithfully in all My wants, so that everything that I suffered in My Body, she suffered in her mind. Thirdly, magnify her, because still in heaven she is most faithful to Me, by gaining for Me sinners so that they may be converted, and souls, so that they may be freed from punishment; for by her intercessions numberless sinners are converted, and by her mercy numberless souls that had been sentenced by a just judgment to long punishment, are called away and freed from the fire of purgatory."

Chapter XXVII.

How the Blessed Mary may be saluted.

DURING the Mass *Salve Sancta parens*, when she was desirous of saluting the Blessed Virgin, our Lord said to her: "Salute My Mother along with every creature." Now as she was thinking how she might do this, she saw the seraphic spirits come from the south, each of them carrying lighted torches. Then, being inspired by God, she understood that these spirits had come alike to minister unto and to help her, and along with these she saluted the Blessed Virgin with the love wherewith she loved God above every creature; with that love, namely, which was so strong within her during the Passion of her only-begotten Son, as utterly to surpass and extinguish all human affection, for while every creature was mourning for the death of the Son of God, she alone, with the Godhead, immoveable and rejoicing, desired her Son to be sacrificed for the world's salvation. Next came the Cherubim with mirrors, whereby she understood that together with these spirits she ought to salute the Blessed Virgin in that most eminent and clear knowledge which above every creature she enjoyed on earth, and by which more clearly than all she now gazeth at the inaccessible light of the Godhead. After this the Thrones brought a throne of ivory, whereby she understood that most peaceful and gentle rest, with which God dwelt in her, and which in every human action, whether flying into Egypt with her Son, or returning therefrom, never could be disturbed even for a moment. The Dominations brought a crown of marvellous beauty, wherein were human heads enamelled with wonderful brilliancy, by which was signified that redemption had come to the human race by the Virgin Mary. The Principalities carried flowering sceptres, wherein she understood that together with these she ought to extol the glorious Virgin for representing the image of God unstained within herself, and more fittingly than every other creature. The Powers had swords, whereby was typified that God had bestowed on her the greatest power in heaven and on earth, over every creature, especially over the demons, who fear her so very much that they cannot bear even the mention of her name. The Virtues had golden cups, from which our Lord poured Himself in gladness, whereby she understood that man should adapt himself to God by virtue, so that God may be able to pour Himself out upon him, and operate in him by His grace. With these spirits also she felt herself bound to salute the glorious Virgin, because in all things she was full of grace and virtues. The Archangels brought an exceeding fair veil, with which they covered both our Lord and His Mother, by which was figured that familiarity between God and the soul, wherewith the most holy Virgin Mary was in a very singular manner endowed on earth. Moreover, the Angels who stood by their King ministered unto her, by which she understood that she herself ought, along with them, to bless God's Mother, and to praise her for all the service which, as His most faithful and devout handmaid, she had ministered unto her Son on earth. After this the Patriarchs and Prophets brought caskets of gold, and they were closed. By this was signified their closed and obscure prophecy, which was fulfilled in the Blessed Virgin and in Christ, and was unlocked for us by the Holy Ghost. The Apostles had splendid books richly ornamented, by which was marked their faithful doctrine, the sound of which hath gone forth unto the ends of the earth; yet these the gentle Virgin far surpassed by the doctrine of her example and virtues. Moreover the Martyrs carried golden shields in their right hand, and roses in their left, signifying by this the victory of suffering, and the constancy of patience, wherewith they had shed their blood for Christ's Name and love, and these, too, the Blessed Virgin surpassed by her constancy and patience. The Confessors, also, offered censers and vials filled with marvellous odours, by which was signified zeal of prayer and of devotion, and amongst these the Blessed Virgin was found first and most excellent. The Virgins, too, carried golden lilies in honour of the Virgin Mother, because by her the illustrious glory of virginity had sprung up on earth. Afterward all the Saints, the very heavens, the earth, and every creature, when called upon together, bowed themselves down towards that happy soul, and offered her the help of their ministry, in order that with them she might worthily salute God's sweet Virgin Mother, who is most worthy of all praise.

Chapter XXVIII.

Of the Salutation of the Blessed Mary.

IT came once into her mind, that she had served our Lady all the days of her life less devoutly than she ought to have done. Then straightway she saw our Lord with the Queen Mother sitting on a lofty throne, and our Lord said unto His Mother: "Arise, My neighbour, and give place to this one." And when the soul heard this, she was sore afraid, and began to think that peradventure this was an illusion. Then our Lord said to her: "Verily, verily, I say unto thee, thou art not deceived, nor ever hast thou been deceived in such things." Then, too, the Blessed Virgin took the soul in her arms, and joined her to the embraces of her own Lover. And our Lord received her with marvellous sweetness, and laid her mouth on His own Divine Heart, and said: "Here shalt thou draw whatever thou wishest to offer to My Mother." And she felt the following little verses, which never before she had either seen or heard, instil themselves into her, as it were, drop by drop: "Hail, most excellent Virgin, in that most sweet droplet, which from everlasting flowed into thee from the Heart of the Most Holy Trinity concerning thy happy predestination!" "Hail, Virgin most holy, in that most sweet droplet, which flowed into thee from the Heart of the Most Blessed Trinity concerning thy happy conversation!" "Hail, Virgin most loving, in that sweet droplet, which flowed into thee from the Most Holy Trinity in the Passion and bitter death of thine only One!" "Hail, Virgin most worthy, in that sweet droplet, which flowed into thee from the Most Blessed Trinity, in all the glory and gladness wherewith thou now rejoicest, and shalt rejoice for ever, elect, and pre-elect over every creature in heaven and on earth, before the foundation of the world!"

Chapter XXIX.

How the Virgin Mary asked that three Ave Marias should be said daily.

ONCE, while she was praying to the gracious Virgin to deign to be present at the hour of her death, our Lady answered: "This indeed will I do, but do thou say to me daily three *Ave Marias*. At the first, pray that, even as God the Father, according to the magnificence of His Omnipotence, hath lifted me up on high to His own most worthy throne, and honoured me with such great honour that after Himself I am the most powerful in heaven and on earth, so I, too, may be present with thee at the hour of death, by strengthening thee, and driving far from thee every power that is opposed to thee. At the second, pray that even, as the Son of God, according to the pre-excellence of His inscrutable Wisdom, hath most cunningly adorned me with knowledge and understanding, and filled me full thereof, so that above all the Saints I enjoy a greater knowledge of the most Blessed Trinity, and that even as He hath lightened me through and through with all brightness, so that as a radiant Sun I light up the whole heaven with my virtue, so, too, at the hour of death, I may pierce through thy soul with the light of faith and knowledge, lest thy faith be tempted through ignorance or aught of error. At the third, pray that, even as the Holy Ghost poured into me the sweetness of His own Love in its fulness, and made me so exceeding gentle and meek, that after our Lord I am the sweetest and the gentlest, so also I may be near thee at the hour of death, by pouring into thy soul the sweetness of the Love of God, and that it may be so exceeding strong in thee, that all the pain and bitterness of death may be to thee, for His Love, exceeding sweet. Amen.

Revelations of S. Mechtild,

VIRGIN,

Taken from the Second Book of her Spiritual Grace.

Chapter I.

How God inviteth the Soul.

ONCE upon a certain Saturday, while the commemoration was being made of God's Virgin Mother, the handmaid of Christ desired to praise her, but knew not with what praise to extol her. Then prostrating herself according to her wont at the feet of Jesus, she saw our Lord, Who had upon His right foot, as it were, a sapphire, and upon the left a granate. Now while she was marvelling at this, our Lord said to her: "Even as the sapphire, by its virtue, driveth out corrupt humours, so do My wounds drive out the virus of the soul, and purify it from all stains.

And as the granate rejoiceth the heart of man, so do My wounds cause the soul, after the correction of her sins, to rejoice in Me." Then rapt out of herself, she saw on high the King of glory, and at His right Hand His imperial Mother, while she herself at His left Hand, rested against His bosom, and listened with attentive ear to the ceaseless and mighty beatings of His own sweet Heart. Moreover, the beatings of the Heart of God sounded like so many invitations which thus spake: "Come and do penance, come and be reconciled, come and be consoled, come and be blessed; come, My love, and receive all that the Beloved can give to His beloved; come, My sister, and possess the inheritance of heaven, which I have bought for thee with My precious Blood; come, My spouse, and enjoy My Godhead."

Now the Virgin Mary had on a vestment of the colour of saffron, on which were red roses, and on these again were golden roses marvellously woven. The saffron colour signified her humility, with which she subjected herself to every creature; the red roses the constancy of the patience with which in all things she was meek and patient, and the golden roses that love of hers, by which she performed all her actions in the love of God. Moreover her under-tunic was green, interwoven with roses of gold, signifying that her whole life had flowered with good works and holy virtues. By the gold was figured love, and that as the tunic was next her body, so love was next her heart. Then that blessed soul saluted the glorious Virgin through the Heart of her Son, and praised her through her Son, with more perfect praise than that with which any creature could praise Him. After this she asked our Lord, that He alone might be lauded in her praise, and that she might never seek anything else except His praise. And our Lord said to her: "Why thinkest thou that it is ordered that the antiphons should be said with heads bowed down, except that the grace, which God poureth out upon the soul, may be received in thanksgiving and praise?" And she saw a tube, as it were, coming out of the Heart of God, to her own heart, and then winding back again from her own heart to that of God, by which was signified the praise of God. Now the tube was studded with golden knots, by which were typified those blessed souls, which praise and glorify our Lord in heaven for ever and for ever.

Chapter II.

Of our Lord's vineyard, which is the Church, and of four kinds of prayer.

ON a certain Sunday, while they were singing the *Asperges me, Domine*, she said: "My Lord, in what wilt Thou now wash and cleanse my heart?" And straightway our Lord with love unutterable embraced her whole being, and said: "In the love of My divine Heart I will wash thee." And He opened the door of His sweet Heart, even the treasure-house of the Godhead, into which she entered as into a vineyard, and she saw therein a river of living water flowing from the east unto the west, and round about the river were twelve trees bearing fruit, that is, the virtues which the blessed Paul enumerateth in his Epistle: charity, joy, peace, patience, longanimity, goodness, benignity, meekness, faith, modesty, continence, chastity. This water is called the river of love; and therefore the soul entered into it, and was washed therein from every stain. In this river there was a multitude of fishes that had golden scales, which signified those loving souls, which, separated from all delights of earth, have plunged themselves in the very well-spring of all good, even in Jesus. In the vineyard there were palm trees, some of which stood erect, while others were bent down to the ground. The palms which stood erect are those who have despised the world with its flowers, and who lift up their minds to heavenly things; and the palms that were bent down are those wretched ones, who lie in the earthly dust of their own thoughts. Moreover our Lord, in the likeness of a gardener, was digging in the earth. And she said to Him: "O Lord, what is Thy spade?" And He answered, "My fear." Now in certain places the earth was hard, in others soft. The hard earth signified the hearts of those who are hardened in sin, and who will not be corrected either by advice or by reproof. The soft earth signified the hearts of those who are softened by tears and true contrition of heart. And our Lord said: "This vineyard is My Catholic Church, in which for thirty and three years I laboured, and which I watered with My sweat; do thou labour with Me in this vineyard." And she said, "How?" And our Lord replied: "By watering it." And straightway the soul ran impetuously to the river, and filled a pail with water, and set it on her shoulders; and as it was exceeding heavy, our Lord came and helped to carry it with her, and its burden became light. And our Lord said: "Thus when I give grace to men, do all things performed or borne for Me seem light and sweet; but when I take away My grace, then do all things seem heavy unto them." Moreover, round about the palms she saw a multitude of angels like unto a wall.

After this the best of masters taught her the Psalm *Miserere mei Deus*, in which there are twenty verses, and how these twenty verses ought to be divided into five and five with the antiphon: "O Blessed and glorious Trinity, Father, Son, and Holy Ghost, have mercy, have mercy, have mercy upon us," and the verse *Miserere*. The first five verses for all sinners who, being hardened in sin, refuse to be converted to God, so that God, by His loving Death, may deign to recal them to Himself by true penance. The second five verses for penitents, that they may obtain the forgiveness they desire, and never go back afresh to their sins. The third five verses for the just, who already are making progress in virtue, so that they may persevere therein. The fourth five verses for all the souls in purgatory, who are certain that before long they will drink in the kingdom of the well of living water, and will reign with Christ for ever, so that they may be the sooner set free, and feast with our Lord. During the Mass, moreover, when the Host was being elevated, our Lord said to her: "Behold, I will give My whole Self, with all the good that is in Me, into thy soul's power, so that whatever thou desirest to do with Me, it is wholly in thy power to do." This she refused to accept, but chose rather in all things to do His will. And our Lord said: "What thou wilt, is in thy power to do." But she, recognizing our Lord's will, said unto Him: "Nothing for my own use do I desire; nothing do I seek, nothing do I wish for, save that to-day Thou shouldst be praised by Thyself and through Thyself, as fitly and perfectly as Thou canst possibly be praised." Then she saw, as it were, a harp go forth from the Heart of God, and it had many chords. Now that harp was our Lord Jesus, and the chords were all the elect, who are one with God in love. Then Jesus Himself, the chief Singer of all the singers, struck the harp; and all the angels chanted with an exceeding sweet sound, and said: "Praise we the King of kings, One God in three Persons, Who hath chosen thee for His daughter and spouse." Then all the Saints sang in God with sweet harmony, and said: "Now give we thanks to God the Father for this harmony with which His grace hath enriched us."

Chapter III.

Of our Lord's Scourge.

ONCE upon a time she saw our Lord standing, holding in His Hand a golden scourge, and threatening her. Then she fell upon the ground, and embraced our Lord's scourge; by which was given her to understand, that man ought with gratitude to receive the gifts of God, whether of prosperity or of adversity. Moreover, our Lord lifted her up, and clothed her with a red tunic full of holes, and said to her: "Thus was all My Body everywhere pierced, and torn with pains, so that from the sole of My Foot to the crown of My Head, there was no sound place in Me." By this was foreshadowed that shortly she was to be oppressed with the trouble of infirmity. She saw, also, our Lord holding behind her a chalice of gold, whereby she understood that the sweetness which God will infuse into the soul is not as yet seen nor tasted, but is hidden in God, from Whom all good things proceed.

Chapter IV.

How our Lord gave her Love to be her Mother.

IT came to pass on a certain day, that Love encompassed her, as it were, with a vesture of sunlight. And there approached two beings, Love, namely, and the soul, and they stood in Christ's presence exceeding fair. Now the soul was very desirous to approach nearer, for although she could contemplate His Imperial Person, yet was not this enough for her. Then Love took the soul and led her to our Lord. And the soul bent herself over the wound of the sweet Heart of her only Saviour, and drank therefrom deep draughts of all deliciousness and sweetness, and all her bitterness was changed therein into sweetness, and her fear into security. She also drew forth from the Heart of Christ an exceeding sweet fruit, which she took from the Heart of God and placed in her own mouth, by which was signified that eternal praise which proceedeth from the Heart of God; for all praise, by which He is Himself praised, floweth forth from Him, Who is the beginning and the end of all good. Then she took another fruit, namely, thanksgiving, for nothing can the soul do of herself, unless she be prevented by God. And our Lord said to her: "Yet one more fruit I desire from thee above all things, namely, that thou shouldst pour out upon Me alone all the delight of thy heart." Then she said: "O my only Beloved, how can I do this?" And He answered: "My love will accomplish it within thee." Then, with exceeding great gratitude, she said: "Ah! even so. Ah! even so, Love." And our Lord said:

"Thou shalt call none other thy mother, and My Love shall be thy mother. And as children suck their mother's breasts, even so shalt thou suck from My Love inward consolation and unutterable health, and My Love shall also feed thee, and clothe thee, and provide for thee in all thy wants, like a mother who provideth for her only daughter."

Chapter V.

How she was made one with her Beloved.

LIKEWISE it came to pass, while she was at prayer, and longing with a fervent heart after the Beloved of her soul, that of a sudden the power of God drew her soul so strongly to Himself, that she seemed to herself to sit down by the side of our Lord. Then our Lord pressed the soul against His Heart in a sweet embrace, and filled her through and through so abundantly with His grace, that she saw rivulets, as it were, flowing forth from all His members upon all the Saints, so that all were penetrated with special joy, and they held in their hands lamps, as it were, exceeding bright, filled with that gift which God had poured out upon the soul, and they returned thanks to our Lord with great gratitude and joy for that soul. Then she saw in the Heart of God, as it were, a virgin, exceeding fair, holding a ring in her hand, on which was a diamond, with which, without intermission, she touched the Heart of God. Moreover, the soul asked why the virgin thus touched the Heart of God. And the virgin answered: "I am Divine Love, and this stone signifieth the sin of Adam. And as the diamond cannot be broken without blood, so the sin of Adam could not be dissolved without the Humanity and Blood of Christ. For straightway, as soon as Adam sinned, I introduced myself and intercepted the whole of his sin, and by thus ceaselessly touching the Heart of God, and moving Him to pity, I suffered Him not to rest until the moment when I took the Son of God from His Father's Heart and laid

Him in His Virgin-Mother's womb. Then I wrapped the Son of God in swaddling clothes, and laid Him in the manger; after this I led Him into Egypt, I moved Him to all that He did and suffered for man, until I fastened Him upon the gibbet of the Cross, and there I softened by every means His Father's wrath, and joined man to God in an indissoluble covenant of love." And the soul said: "Tell me, I pray thee, of all the things which Christ suffered for us, which was the one in which He suffered most?" And Love answered: "When He was so stretched out upon the Cross, that all His bones could be numbered. Whosoever returneth thanks to Him for this, payeth Him as sweet homage as if He had mollified His wounds with exceeding sweet ointment. So also, if a man return thanks for the thirst wherewith upon the Cross He thirsted for man's salvation, He will receive it as if He had refreshed His thirst. Moreover, whosoever shall return thanks to Him for having hung nailed upon the Cross, it will be as grateful to Him as if he had loosened Him from the Cross and freed Him from all pains." And again Love said unto the soul: "Enter into the joy of thy Lord." At this she was wholly rapt into God, so that as a drop of water poured into wine is wholly changed into wine, even so did this blessed soul pass into God, as if she had been made one spirit with Him. And God comforted her, and said: "All that ever man can receive will I pour into thee, and as far as it is possible for man, will I multiply My gifts upon thee." And Love said: "Here take thy rest, and repose in the Heart of thy Lover, lest ever thou shouldst be disquieted in prosperity. Here rest in remembrance of the good things which God, thy Beloved, hath done for thee, lest ever thou shouldst be disquieted in adversity."

Chapter VI.

How God adorneth the Soul with holy virtues.

ON a certain day, while the Psalm *Laudate Dominum de cœlis* was being read, at the words: *Et aquæ quæ super cœlos sunt laudent nomen Domini*, she said to our Lord: "O Lord, what are these waters of which we here sing?" And He answered: "They are all the tears of the Saints, which they have ever shed out of love, or devotion, or compassion, or contrition." And straightway she saw that the water which signified the tears of the Saints was exceeding clear, and that its bottom was of most pure gold, having for sand pearls and precious stones, whereby were typified the divers virtues of the Saints, in which they had exercised themselves on earth, namely, prayers, vigils, and other works of zeal. And there was a multitude of fish in the water, playing and moving themselves about, by which were signified the desires which move the soul towards God, and the sighs and plaints whereby the soul attracteth God towards herself. For the Saints in heaven contemplate their own virtues, and all their good works in God, for the increase of their joys, and the delight of their heart, although each one in himself hath glory in his own virtues.

After this she complained unto our Lord that she had not celebrated the day of her espousals as devoutly, nor cleaved unto Him with as great fidelity, as a bride ought to have done with regard to her only Bridegroom. Then our Lord clad her in a vesture of His own most perfect virtues, and He placed on her head a diadem of gold, and pressed her to Him in the embrace of love; and He put His arm round about her. But when the soul marvelled at this, our Lord said to her: "Between Me and thee there is no darkness." She saw, also, thousands upon thousands of angels standing with reverence before Christ the King. And our Lord said unto the soul: "Lo! all these do I give unto thee, to serve thee." But she desired that all the ministry they rendered her might show forth the praise and glory of her only Lover. Then straightway she saw tubes, as it were, going forth from the hearts of the angels to the Heart of God, and they made such sweet melody that no man can utter it. After this the Heart of Christ opened Itself, and He Himself entered into it, and shut her therein together with Himself, saying unto her thus: "The upper part of My Heart will be for thee the sweetness of the Spirit of God, and continually will it keep dropping into thy soul. To this wilt thou lift up thine eyes with panting desire, and thou wilt open thy mouth to draw in the sweetness of God's grace, as it is said in the psalm: '*I opened my mouth, and drew in Thy Spirit.*' In the lower part thereof thou shalt find the treasury of all good, and the overflowing abundance of desirable things. On the eastern side thou shalt find the light of true knowledge, for understanding and accomplishing all My Will. On the south side thou shalt see the paradise of eternal riches; there thou shalt ever sit with Me at table."

And straightway she saw a table set therein, and a cloth exceeding fair laid upon it. By the table was signified bounty, by the cloth piety. At the table our Lord sat, and the soul ministered to Him with joy many courses; that is to say, she set before Him divers gifts of God. For as often as she returned thanks for the Divine bounty, for each of God's gifts and for His numberless benefits, so often she placed a course before Him. And she said to our Lord: "What do I offer Thee, O my Beloved, when I pray for my friends?" He answered: "Thou offerest Me wine exceeding generous, that filleth My Heart with joy." And the soul said: "What do I offer Thee when I pray for sinners?" He answered: "Thou offerest Me wine exceeding sweet, sweeter than honey and the honey-comb, when thou prayest for My enemies, who are in a state of damnation, that they may be converted unto Me." And the soul asked: "What do I offer Thee, when I pray for the [Holy]

Souls?" He answered: "Thou offerest Me wine which also gladdeneth My Heart, when thou prayest for those who are in My good will, that they may be the sooner delivered from their pains." Then the soul said: "O most loving One! how fervently do I now desire to offer Thee my heart." And straightway He took her heart into His Hands, and smelt it, as if it had been a sweet-smelling rose. And the soul said to Him: "What fragrance dost Thou perceive therein, in which is no good thing?" And our Lord answered: "When I am in thy soul, I perceive the sweetness of Myself." After this He said to her: "On the western side are length of days, eternal peace, and joy without end. On the northern side thou shalt receive eternal security, whereby thou shalt overcome all thy enemies, so that no adversary shall any more prevail against thee."

Chapter VII.

How our Lord's Heart was seen under the similitude of a lamp.

DURING a certain Mass when, in consequence of divers distracting thoughts, she was deprived of the enjoyment of God's presence, she prayed to the Blessed Virgin Mary, and besought her to obtain for her the presence of her beloved Son. And by her intercession, as she believed, she beheld the King of glory, our Lord Jesus, sitting on a high throne, which was transparent with crystal purity. And from the front of the throne there went forth two little streams of exceeding great purity, and these she understood to be the grace of the forgiveness of sins, and of that of spiritual consolation, which, during Mass, are given to every one in a more special and easy manner. Moreover, about the Elevation of the Blessed Host, our Lord rose up from the throne, and seemed to elevate with His own Hands His own most Sacred Heart, as it were a lamp, exceeding bright, full, and overflowing. Now this lamp, on every side and all round about it, overflowed with such vehemence, that large drops leaped out above the flowing stream, and yet the fulness of the lamp did not seem in anywise to be lessened. By this it was given her to understand, that although grace is ministered more than sufficiently out of the fulness of Christ's Heart to all, yet in Himself it overfloweth with great exuberance in all blessedness, nor doth it ever in anywise suffer decrease. Moreover she saw the hearts of all present fastened, as it were, to the Heart of our Lord, by little strings of lamps; some of which seemed to stand upright, and to be full of oil, while others were empty, and hung upside down; wherefore she understood that by the lamps that burnt upright were signified the hearts of those who were present at Mass with devotion and longing desires, while by the lamps that hung down were signified the hearts of those who refused to be raised up by devotion. Then with a great desire she longed that her own heart might be wholly plunged into the Heart of God: and straightway she knew that it was lifted up out of the midst of the others, and plunged into the Divine Heart.

After this she saw the Divine Heart changed into an exceeding fair house, in which she saw four fair virgins, that is, four virtues, humility, patience, meekness and charity, which appeared—as indeed they often did—in green vestments. And as she wondered at this, our Lord said: "In as much as charity causeth many dry trunks, that is, sinners, to grow green again by its power, and to flower again and bring forth the fruit of good works, for this reason it is just that the virtues should appear dressed in green." And our Lord added: "Try to fit thyself for familiarity with these virgins, and form friendships with them, if thou desirest to abide with Me in this My house, and to enjoy My presence. By the grace of the Word, when vanity dissolveth thy heart cultivate the virtue of charity, which took

Me from My rest in My Father's Bosom, and placed Me in the Virgin's womb, and wrapped Me in vile swaddling clothes, and laid Me in the manger, and compelled Me to suffer many labours in preaching, and, last of all, killed Me by an exceeding bitter and shameful death. The remembrance of such things will utterly take away all vanity from thy heart. In like manner, when pride troubleth thee, call to mind My Humility, for never even in the least thought, or word, or deed, was I proud, but I showed forth an example of perfect humility in all My Saints. So wilt thou overcome pride by humility. Moreover, when impatience annoyeth thee, remember My patience in poverty, hunger, thirst, in many journeyings, in contumelies, and, above all, in death. So, likewise, when thou art troubled by anger, call to mind My meekness, how I was peaceful and meek with those who hated peace, nay, so much so, that even for My very crucifiers, who, when they had tried every kind of cruelty, and could add nothing more, still in their exceeding fury gnashed at Me with their teeth, I asked for pardon, and appeased the Father for them, with as great sweetness of heart as if they had never gone against Me; and so wilt thou be able to overcome all vices by virtues."

After this, when once upon a time the Congregation went in procession to meet a certain funeral, this handmaid of God allowed herself to look at the fields of the broad plain, and having taken great pleasure therein, she said to our Lord: "My Lord, what sin have I committed in thus looking about me, and taking delight in the broad fields?" He answered: "Thou hast sinned against obedience, and hast not attended to Me; moreover, thou hast neglected to pray for the soul of him who is dead." And she said: "Teach me, O most loving One, how we ought to do for the future, if we should happen to go out." He answered: "First, when ye have gone out of the choir, read the versicle *Deduc me Domine*—'Lead me, O Lord, in Thy way, and I will walk in Thy truth; let my heart rejoice so as to fear Thy Name.' Go out thus in My fear, and take Me for the companion of thy journey, and also My staff, as it were, that ye, going forth in the way, may both support yourselves, and bless the houses, and the way itself, and all who meet you, with My Right Hand, yea, and they shall be blessed. For when a man hath vain joy, according to his own heart, afterwards he is burdened; but he who hath My fear shall not be made sad, but shall obtain true joy. Then, when ye come nigh unto the funeral, ye can call to mind that great procession, in which on the judgment-day all shall rise with their bodies, and come to meet Me, and in which I Myself, girt about with glory and majesty unutterable, shall go to meet them with the multitude of all the Angels and the Saints. Ye shall pray also for the soul of him who is dead, that if he is in punishment he may be the sooner loosened, or if he is kept away from Me by some impediment, he may be freed therefrom, so that in joy and glory he may be presented to Me on that tremendous day."

Chapter VIII.

Of the Cross and our Lord's silken vestment.

ONCE upon a time, being in like manner rapt in spirit, she saw herself, as it were, in a certain house of marvellous beauty, which well she knew was the Heart of Christ. And falling on the ground she found a large cross upon the pavement, and she sank down upon it; and lo! from the middle of the cross there went forth a golden spear and transfixed her. And she heard our Lord saying unto her: "All the substance of earth could not make glad one soul, but all her salvation and highest glory consisteth in pains and tribulations." Then the soul began to be exceeding sad and troubled, in that, although she heard her only Beloved, yet she saw Him not. And when she sought Him with great longing, straightway He appeared to her, standing before her, clad in a vestment of silk, and it was red. And He took her hand, and spoke to her most sweetly. Now when the soul felt the exceeding softness and smoothness of this vestment, she began to think what was signified thereby. And our Lord said unto her: "Even as the silken vestment is smooth and soft, so is all pain and all tribulation sweet to the soul that truly loveth God." And the soul said: "At the beginning of the pain this is so, when the soul toucheth it with exceeding great desire; but when the pain has grown stronger, it will become to her very burdensome." To this He answered: "True; but as a silken vestment, when it is adorned with gold and precious stones, is never thrown aside or hated on account of the heaviness, but is ennobled thereby, and held all the dearer, even so the soul that is faithful will not refuse pain on account of its bitterness, for all her virtues are ennobled thereby, and all her reward is infinitely increased."

Chapter IX.

Of her threefold pain.

ACCORDING to the multitude of His consolation and sweetness, God also multiplieth pains and infirmities in the soul that loveth Him, as the faithful soul of whom we are speaking has often experienced. For once upon a time, for more than a month, she suffered from a very grave weakness of the head, on account of which she was unable to take any sleep or any rest; moreover, also, she lost all her wonted grace and sweetness and the visitation of God, so that she often complained with tears that she could not even think sweetly of God; and for this reason she fell into such a state of sadness, that at times she cried out in her misery after God her Beloved One, and the sound of her cries was heard throughout the whole house. But when she had remained in this desolation more than seven days, our most gracious Lord, Who is ever nigh unto those who are of a troubled heart, poured out upon her and through her such abundant consolation and sweetness, that often, from Matins to Prime, and from Prime to None, she remained lost in the enjoyment of God, with her eyes closed, like unto a woman who is dead, during which space of time our kind Lord revealed unto her the wonders of His secrets, and gladdened her greatly with the sweetness of His presence, so that being no longer able to contain herself, she poured forth, like one who is drunk with wine, that interior grace which for so many years she had kept hidden, upon all who came to her, even upon guests and strangers. Wherefore, many communicated their affairs to her, to each of whom, as God deigned to disclose them, she made known the desires of their hearts, and they being glad thereat returned thanks to God. So then her soul dwelt in the Divinity like a fish in the water or a bird in the air. Moreover, it came to pass that S. Peter appeared to her, as if gazing on her with wonder that the Lord of

Majesty should bow down in such condescension to her soul. And our Lord said to S. Peter: "Why dost thou marvel, Peter, for both the first and the last of My children are to Me exceeding dear? You were My first begotten disciples, to whom I showed all benevolence, and all that you wished for you had in Me, according to the desires of your hearts."

After this, as she was praying for the Congregation, she heard an exceeding sweet sound re-echoing in the firmament of heaven from the sound of the disciplines, which at that hour the sisters took for their common salvation. At the sound the holy Angels clapped their hands, and leapt for joy, the devils who were tormenting souls fled far away, the holy souls were loosened from their pains, and the chains of their sins were broken.

Chapter X.

How she gave all the Saints to drink of the Well of Mercy.

AGAIN, on another night, she asked of our Lord in what place it was His will that she should pass the night. And He answered: "At the foot of this desert mountain." Then she saw a well of mercy thereon, and over it little shields of silver. And our Lord said: "Give to drink out of this well to all and each of the Saints, according to thy will." To which she replied: "Do Thou, I beseech of Thee, O my Lord, supply my place, for I am not fit for this work, since I am weak, and infirm." Then the holy angels, taking her place, gave to drink out of that well, first of all, to the glorious Virgin Mary, for the increase of all her beatitude; and as she drank, each drop sounded so sweetly in her throat, that all the citizens of the blessed Jerusalem burst forth into new excellent jubilee. Then they gave the Patriarchs to drink, and the Prophets, and the Apostles, and the Martyrs, and the Confessors, and the Virgins, and the widows, and the married, and all the citizens of heaven, who all, in like manner, drank thereof; and each drop they drank sounded most sweetly to God's praise. Next they gave to drink out of the well aforesaid, first of all, to the Apostolic Lord, to the Cardinals, Archbishops, Bishops, and all the religious orders; after these to the Emperor, the Kings and Princes, and lastly, to all who were alive upon the earth, and likewise to the souls in purgatory. All, indeed, drank thereof, but not all tasted the same sweetness as had been enjoyed by the Church Triumphant.

Chapter XI.

How she was called by God together with Love, and of the psaltery of ten chords.

ANOTHER time, having been sweetly called to our Lord Jesus, she saw how Love, under the likeness of a fair virgin, went round about the consistory, singing: "*Alone I have made the circuit of heaven, and I have walked on the waves of the sea.*" In these words she understood how Love had subjected to herself the Omnipotence of God's Majesty, and had made, as it were, drunken His unsearchable Wisdom, and had poured forth all His most sweet Goodness, and by wholly conquering His Divine Justice, and changing it into gentleness and mercy, had moved the Lord of Majesty to come down to the exile of our misery. At the words also, "*And I walked on the waves of the sea,*" she understood how all who before the Law and under the Law had clung unto God in their tribulations faithfully through love, had conquered all adversity and vice by means of love.

Then again Love sang: "He who sitteth on the globe heareth." By which she understood how all the Saints in jubilee see now all the great things which our Lord has done in them; namely, with what inestimable Wisdom He had elected them, how freely He had justified them, and made them worthy by His grace, with how mighty and strong a love He had freed them from every misery, and had turned, not only all good things, but even evil things, to their advantage and salvation. And this praise God accepteth as gratefully from the Saints, as if not from Him, but from themselves they had all these great and good things, and yet to Him alone gave the glory.

Again, it seemed to her as if Love stood at the Right Hand of God, from Whose Heart there went forth a certain musical instrument of an exceeding sweet sound, and it stretched forth to the heart of that virgin who held a psaltery of ten chords, as is said in the psalm: "On the psaltery of ten strings will I praise Thee." By the ten strings are marked the nine choirs of Angels, and the Sanctifier of all the Saints. Then the soul fell down before our Lord, and lightly touching the first string she praised God, and said: "Thee God the Father unbegotten;" on the second she said: "Thee the Son Only-begotten;" on the third: "Thee the Holy Ghost, the Comforter;" on the fourth: "Holy and Undivided Trinity;" on the fifth: "With our whole heart and mouth we confess;" on the sixth: "We praise;" on the seventh: "And bless;" on the eighth: "To Thee be glory;" on the ninth: "For evermore." On the tenth string she could not sing, for as yet she could not reach up to the heights of God. After this she desired that all in heaven and on earth might be made partakers of Divine grace, and taking our Lord's Hand, she made so large a sign of the Cross, that it seemed to take in the heavens and the earth. By this the joy of the inhabitants of heaven was increased, pardon was given to the guilty, comfort to the sad, strength and perseverance to the just, while upon the souls in purgatory was bestowed absolution and alleviation of pains.

Chapter XII.

Of the Title and usefulness of this Book.

ALMOST the whole of this book hath been written by a person who was familiar with the servant of God, and to whom she was wont to reveal her secrets. It was also written in such a way as that she should not know about it. But when she had learnt this from a certain one, she was made so exceeding sad, that in no way could she be at all consoled. Wherefore fleeing, as was her wont, to our Lord, she laid open before Him her sadness with confidence. Our Lord said to her: "My Bride, in the freedom of My sweet and bountiful Heart, and in My Goodness, have I shown and revealed these things." And she said: "What will become of this book after my death, or what use will spring from it, and what shall be the name or title of the book?" He answered her: "All who search therein with faithfulness of heart, shall be made glad therein, and they who love Me shall grow more burning in My Love, and they who are sad shall find in it consolation. Moreover, it shall be called the Book of Spiritual Grace."

Now all the things which are here written are, as it were, but few in comparison with those that have been omitted. For many things were often revealed to her by our Lord, which she would never tell. Nay, sometimes, so spiritual was the revelation, that it seemed as if in no way it could be explained in words.

Revelations of S. Mechtild,

VIRGIN,

Taken from the Third Book of her Spiritual Grace.

Chapter I.

Of the Ring set with seven stones.

ONE day, when the Virgin of Christ felt not the presence of her Beloved, and greatly longed for it, she seemed to see, as it were, our Lord standing before her, and that they both spoke many things together. While then they were singing at Mass: *Et tibi reddetur votum in Hierusalem,* she thought how many vows the Saints had offered to our Lord in this world,—the Blessed Virgin and the other virgins their chastity, the Martyrs their precious blood, and the other Saints many labours and much devotion, and she grieved that she herself had nothing that she could offer. Then she saw the Blessed Virgin standing at her right hand, who gave her a ring of gold, which straightway she offered to our Lord, and which our Lord thankfully received and placed upon His finger. Considering this within herself, she said: "Oh! if it could be, that He Himself should give His own ring to thee, as a sign of espousal." And it seemed to her that it would be enough if our Lord would deign to give her a pain in her ring-finger, which she would wish to bear all the days of her life, in memory that Christ had espoused her. Our Lord said to her: "I give to thee a ring set with seven stones, which thou canst call to mind on the seven joints of thy finger. On the first joint thou canst call to mind My Divine Love, which drew Me down from My Father's bosom, and caused Me to serve thirty and three years in seeking after thee. And when the time of My nuptials was at hand, I was Myself sold by My own Heart's love as the price of the marriage-banquet, and I gave Myself for bread, and flesh, and drink. In like manner, at the banquet, I Myself was the harp and the organ, by means of the sweet words of My mouth; and to joyfully entertain the guests, after the manner of sports, I humbled Myself at the feet of the disciples. On the second joint thou shalt call to mind what kind of dance I, Who was so exceeding fair, performed after the banquet, when three times I fell upon the ground, and made, as it were, three such powerful bounds, that all dripping with bloody sweat I shed great drops of blood. In that dance I clothed all My fellow-soldiers in threefold garments, when I obtained for them the forgiveness of their sins, the sanctification of their souls, and My Divine enlightenment. On the third, thou shalt remember the love of My humility at the kiss of the bride, when the betrayer came near and kissed Me, at which kiss My Heart felt such strong love pass through it, that had his soul repented, I would have taken it by that kiss to be My bride. For then I joined to Myself all the souls, which from everlasting I had predestined to be My brides. On the fourth, call to mind what kind of marriage songs My ears listened to for the love of My Bride, when I stood before the judge, and so much false witness was brought forward against Me. On the fifth, remember how becomingly, for thy love, I adorned Myself, when so many times I changed My vestments, for white and purple and scarlet were My vestments, and for a garland of roses I wore a crown of thorns. On the sixth, be mindful how I embraced thee, when I was bound to the column: there, for thy sake, I received upon Me the darts of all thine enemies. On the seventh, be mindful how I entered the marriage-bed of the Cross. And as spouses give their bridal clothes to actors, so did I give My vestments to the soldiers, and My Body to them who crucified Me. Then I stretched out My arms, by means of the cruel nails, for thy sweet embraces, singing on My bed of love seven long songs of marvellous sweetness. After this I opened My Heart for thee to enter in, even when in dying on the Cross I slept with thee the sleep of love."

Chapter II.

Of the Rose which went forth out of the Heart of God.

DURING a certain Mass, she said to our Lord: "O most loving One, teach me how to praise Thee!" Our Lord said to her: "Look at My Heart." And lo! an exceeding fair rose, having five leaves, went forth from God's Heart, and covered all His breast. And our Lord said: "Praise Me for My five senses, which are signified by this rose." Then she understood that she ought to praise our Lord for His praiseworthy and loving sight, by which He looketh ever on man, even as a father on his only son, never giving way to wrath, but ever regarding him as a friend, as if wishing and desiring that man should always have recourse to Him. Secondly, for His hearing, by which

His ear is ever bowed down and attentive, so that at the least whisper or groan of men He is more delighted than at many songs from the Angels. Thirdly, for His smell, by which He hath ever a living liking for man, and by which He exciteth the heart of man to delight in Him, for no man can take delight in a good word, unless he be prevented by God. And this is why it is written: "My delights are to be with the children of men." Fourthly, for the exceeding sweet taste which is found in the Mass, where He Himself is the soul's sweet food. And in this food He so incorporateth the soul with Himself, that by this union with God the soul is made the food of God. Fifthly, for the loving touch, by which Love touched Him bitterly upon the Cross, fixing the nails in His Hands and Feet, and the spear into His Side; and even as at the time the soul of whom we are writing was transfixed with grief beyond compare, so now she still remains marked in her hands, and feet, and heart with unutterable jubilee of love, so that not even for a moment can she forget it.

Chapter III.

That God ought to be praised in three ways.

IN like manner she saw our Lord surrounded with unutterable glory; and He had on His breast a leaf of clear silver, round about which were chasings beyond all price, on which were represented the sufferings of each of the Saints, which they had undergone for Christ. For in the glory of God the Saints contemplate all their good deeds and their own dignities, because there is nothing so small that they have done for His love, or suffered in thought, word, or deed, for which they will not receive an everlasting reward, while they themselves will glorify God for all His gifts. And she said to our Lord: "O most sweet and loving One! in what is it most Thy pleasure that I should exercise myself?" He answered her: "In praise." She said: "Teach me, then, that worthily I may praise Thee." Then our Lord taught her three ways, as it were three beats of music, and said: "First thou shalt praise the Omnipotence of the Father, by which, in the Son and in the Holy Ghost, He worketh according to His Will, and Him, no creature, however immense, whether in heaven or in earth, can contain. Next thou shalt praise the inscrutable Wisdom of the Son, which He communicateth fully, together with the Father and the Holy Ghost, according to His Will, which no creature can fully grasp. Lastly, thou shalt praise the graciousness of the Holy Ghost, which, together with the Father and the Son, He abundantly communicateth according to all His Will, in which, also, no creature can fully share. The second way, or beat, is that in which thou oughtest to praise Me for every grace and gift that flowed out of the abundance of My goodness upon My Virgin Mother, who was more abundantly filled with every grace and good, than ever was any other creature. Give thanks, also, for every grace given to all the Saints who now stand in the presence of My Majesty and gladness, and gaze with jubilee upon Me, the Well-spring of all good. The third way is, that thou oughtest to praise Me for every grace and gift that flowed forth from Me upon all mankind: upon the good, whom I sanctify and confirm by My grace; upon sinners, whom I invite to penance, and from whom I mercifully wait for good; and also upon all the souls, which, by My grace, I daily loose from purgatory, and lead into the joys of heaven." At the first beat, it seemed to her that she ought to say: "To Thee be glory;" at the second: "Rightly they praise Thee;" at the third: "From Whom are all things." After this, in accordance with the desire of the soul, the ornament which was on the breast of her Lover Jesus divided itself, and the soul entered into the sweet Heart of Christ, and there being made, as it were, one spirit with her Beloved, beyond doubt tasted and saw what it is not lawful for men to utter.

Chapter IV.

How man should salute the Heart of God.

THERE once appeared to the servant of Christ an angel of the Lord, who drew from her heart, as it were, a scroll, on which were written in her own blood the words: "God is faithful, and in Him there is no iniquity." And also: "I would rather die than be separated from Thee by sin;" and this scroll he joyfully presented to our Lord. Now in the morning, having been troubled with distractions, she had, in resisting them, thought of these words, and the Angel said to her: "To day thou hast thought of these words. Know, then, that as often as a man, in resisting his thoughts and desires, resolveth rather to die than to consent to sin, straightway this will be accepted before God, as if that man had carried out that resolution into effect." Then, falling down at the feet of our Lord, she complained that she had wasted the whole time of her life in useless living, and resolved that for the future, if it were possible for her to live until the last judgment-day, she would wish to live in the greatest pains and sorrows in which ever man hath lived upon the earth. And our Lord said to her: "For all that thou hast neglected, salute My Heart in the Divine goodness, for it is the well-spring and origin of all good, and from it all good proceedeth. Secondly, salute My Heart in the exuberance of grace which hath flowed therefrom, still floweth, and will flow upon all the Saints, and the souls of such as are to be saved. Thirdly, salute that sweet vein of My most tender Heart, which so often hath burst and poured itself out upon thy soul, and inebriated it with the torrent of My Divine pleasure."

Chapter V.

How a man should live in accordance with God's good pleasure.

AGAIN, it came to pass on a certain day, that it seemed to her as if a dove sat on the bosom of our Lord, which signified the simple, who receive the gifts of God with a simple heart, and neither discuss the works of God or of man, and in these God taketh exceeding great delight. Now, when she desired to know how she ought to rule herself, she understood that it should be according to the conversation of Christ, which was divided into four parts. For, first, Christ was fervent of heart; so too, she herself, when alone, ought always to keep her mind fixed on the consideration of His Godhead, or on the operation of His Humanity, or in meditating on what God has done in His Saints, or in all those on whom He has poured out His mercy. Secondly, Christ was friendly and gentle to all, doing no harm to any man by a biting word. So, too, ought her word always to have to do with the actions of Christ, or the examples of the Saints, or the utility of her neighbours. Thirdly, Christ was of use in all' His works in the healing of the body, as well as in the healing of the soul. So, too, ought she to try to perform all her works zealously, with a prudent and merry heart. Fourthly, Christ was most patient in all His persecutions and sufferings: so she also ought to be patient with regard to all pains and injuries; bearing them with gentleness. As a sheep which is at pasture keepeth always bleating, but when dragged to be butchered is dumb: so, when it perceiveth no grievance, ought the faithful soul to fear, and when troubled in body or soul, to feel always safe. Then she prayed our Lord to instruct her how to live each hour according to His good pleasure. Our Lord said to her: "In the morning, when thou risest, offer thy heart to Me, in order that I may pour into it My Divine Blood. At the Mass thou oughtest to be with Me, as if at a banquet, where all meet together and none is excepted, but where all bring with them their own provisions, that is, their prayers. At that banquet I, the Lord, enrich poverty with the liberality of the divine majesty of all virtues, and take away the afflictions of all." And the soul said: "Tell me what Thou doest when I pray or read psalms." Our Lord said to her: "I listen; and when thou workest, I rest, and the more zealously thou labourest, the more sweetly do I repose in thee. When thou eatest, I labour, for thou feedest on Me, and I on thee; when thou sleepest, I watch and guard thee."

CHAPTER VI.

How man should salute the Heart of God.

ON the morning, when first thou risest, salute the flowering and loving Heart of thy sweet Lover, from which all good, all joy, all happiness hath flowed forth in heaven and on earth, still floweth forth, and shall flow forth for ever, and endeavour to plunge thine own heart therein with the whole strength of thy heart, and say: "I praise, bless, magnify, glorify, and salute the most sweet Heart of Jesus Christ, my most faithful Lover; I give thanks to Thee for the faithful guardianship with which Thou hast protected me during this night, and hast ceaselessly paid for me to God the Father, all the praise and thanksgiving, and all that I owed Him. And now, O only Beloved of my soul, I offer Thee my heart as a flowering rose, the pleasantness of which may attract Thine eyes the whole day, and the fragrance of which may delight Thy Divine Heart. I offer Thee, also, my heart, that Thou mayest use it as a cup, from which Thou mayest drink the sweetness of Thine own Self, together with all that Thou mayest deign to work in me during this day. Moreover, I offer Thee my heart as a pomegranate, of exceeding sweet savour, and fit for Thy royal banquet, by eating which Thou mayest so transfer it into

Thyself, that for the future it may happily feel itself within Thee; and, at the same time, I pray that every thought, word, work, and all my will may be this day directed according to the good pleasure of Thy most gracious Will." And our Lord added: "Then sign thyself with the sign of the Cross, and say: 'In the Name of the Father, and of the Son, and of the Holy Ghost. Holy Father, in union with the Love of Thy most loving Son, I commend to Thee my spirit.' Repeat this word at each of thy actions, when thou beginnest them, or when thou enterest the choir, and beginnest the Hours, or when thou wishest to pray; and have confidence in God, that the work which thou art then doing can never perish. Commend, also, thy sight, both inward and outward, to the Wisdom of God, and pray that He may give thee the light of knowledge, whereby thou mayest be able to recognize and fulfil His Will, and all His good pleasure. Thy hearing, too, commend to the Divine Mercy, that it may give thee understanding of all the things which thou art to hear during the day, and guard thee from seeing and hearing what is hurtful to thee. Thy mouth, also, and thy voice, commend to God's faithfulness, and pray that He may pour into thee the taste of His own Divine Spirit, whereby all that thou mayest utter during the day may have for thee a good savour, and that He may open thy mouth to praise and give Him thanks, and guard thee from all sin. Moreover, commend thy hands to God's fatherly care, and pray that He may sanctify and fulfil thy works, and draw thee away from every evil deed. Thy heart, also, commend to God's love, and pray that He may draw it with all sweetness into His own Heart, and so set it on fire with His love, that never more may it be able to feel earthly joy or delight. In like manner, at Mass, offer thy heart to God, and before the Secret, cleanse, prepare and free it from all earthly things, that it may be able to receive the outflowing of the Heart of God, which ceaselessly influenceth and filleth the hearts of all present.

Chapter VII.

What man should do to atone for his negligences, and how our Lord cometh in seven ways at the Mass.

ANOTHER time, as she was praying to our Lord for a certain person, and was inquiring of Him what He would accept in satisfaction for her negligences, she received the following answer from our Lord: "Let her say thrice the Psalm '*Laudate Dominum omnes gentes.*' Once in the morning let her say it, and let her take the true Jesus in her right hand, and present Him to God the Father, together with all the works of His Infancy and Boyhood, to supply for all the good actions she neglected to perform in her childhood. Let her read it a second time at Mass, and taking Jesus, her Lord, as the Spouse of her soul, let her accuse herself before God of never having shown either love or fidelity or due reverence to so great a

Spouse, and let her call to mind how many good things she hath freely received from Him, when she was poor and nothing at all, and yet how He hath made her abound in all good things. Then let her offer to God the Father that most burning Love which bloomed in Christ, together with all virtue, during His glorious youth."

Then, remembering her own poverty, she said to our Lord: " Ah! how poor and vile a spouse I am, who would not have had even a ring wherewith to plight Thee my troth, had I not received it from Thee." Straightway, He showed her a ring of so great a size, that it encircled both our Lord and the soul, and it had on it seven precious gems. By these seven gems she understood to be signified the seven ways in which our Lord deigneth to come in the Mass. The first way is that in which our Lord cometh in such great lowliness, that there is no one present so wicked, to whom He will not humbly bow Himself down and come to him, if so be that the wicked man desireth Him. The second way is that in which He cometh with such great patience, that there is no sinner there or enemy of His, whom He will not patiently bear with, and if he desire to be reconciled with Him, gladly forgive him all his debts. The third way is that in which He cometh in the Mass, with such great love that there is no one present so cold and obstinate, whom He is not able, if that man desireth it, to inflame with His love and soften his heart. The fourth way is that in which He cometh with such bountiful liberality, that there is none so poor, whom He cannot abundantly enrich. The fifth way is that in which He offereth Himself to all as such sweet, and delicious, and all-sufficing food, that there is none so sick or so hungry there, who may not be refreshed by Him, and abundantly satisfied. The sixth way is that in which He cometh with such brightness, that there is no one whose heart is so blind and darkened that it cannot be enlightened and purified by His Presence. The seventh way is that in which He cometh in the Mass so full of holiness and grace, that there is none present so slothful and indevout, who may not be roused from his torpor and lukewarmness, and stirred up to devotion.

Again, a third time, let her read once the psalm "*Laudate Dominum.*" Let her read it at Vespers, and taking her Lord Jesus, and with Him all His perfect conversation, let her present Him to God the Father for all the negligences of her life, praying that by Him full satisfaction may be made for all her imperfections. Moreover, if she desire sufficiently to recover all that she hath lost, or vitiated, or neglected, let her often approach to the most noble and worthy Sacrament of Christ's Body, Which containeth in Itself all good, and is the source in which all grace is to be found.

Chapter VIII.

How man may drive away sloth.

ONCE in the summer time, when this pious and devout virgin was yearning in a wonderful way after heavenly things, she saw certain of the sisters slothful and asleep at Mass, and burning with zeal for justice, and at the same time carried away by the love of piety, she said to our Lord: "Ah! Lord God, why is it that wretched man is so weak, that even when he is present at the Divine Mysteries, he cannot keep from sleep?" To this our Lord made answer: "If men thought of heavenly things, or even of the pains of hell, they would drive away sleep far from them." And she said: "To those to whom it is not given to do this, what ought they to do?" He answered: "If a man had a friend who was very dear to him, he would grieve if he were kept far away from friendly intercourse with him. Whosoever therefore thinketh how faithful and loving a friend I am, when he shall come to Me I will open to him all my secrets, so that he will wish or desire to know nothing else, and his heart will be justly stirred up to take delight in Me. Moreover, whosoever shall think how I shall be to him the sweetness of every taste, according to all the desire of his heart, and how powerful and free he himself will be in My free bounty, the thought of this will deservedly drive away sleep from such a man. Wherefore, let a man receive with gratitude all the gifts of God, and give thanks for each, and from day to day make progress in virtue, until he abound in every good."

Chapter IX.

Of the threefold unguent of love.

ONCE, when she had prayed for a certain person, who had complained to her that she felt no devotion in communicating, she gave her the following doctrine from God: "When thou desirest to communicate, if thou feelest thy heart lukewarm with regard to prayer, nor hast any desire or love, as it becometh thee to have, cry with thy whole heart to God, and say: 'Draw me after Thee, we will run to the odour of Thy ointments.' At the word 'draw,' think how mighty and immense hath been that love, which hath led the Almighty and Eternal God to so shameful a punishment as that of the Cross; and desire that He Who said, 'If I shall be lifted up from the earth, I will draw all things unto Me,' may draw thy heart, with all the powers of thy soul, to Himself, and make thee to run with love and desire to the odour of those ointments which have flowed in such abundance from the noble spice-chest of His Heart, that they have filled heaven and earth. The first unguent is made of water of roses, which Divine Love extracted from the noblest of all roses, namely, our Lord's breast, in the still of charity. Use this unguent to wash the face of thy soul, and think diligently, if thou findest any stain of sin, how thou mayest pray and desire that it should be washed away in the fountain of His mercy wherein He washed the thief upon the Cross. The second unguent is that ruby wine, namely, His most holy Blood, which the wine-press pressed out upon the Cross, and brought forth together with water from His Heart's rosy wound; and ask that thy face may be coloured therewith, so that thou mayest be rendered fit and worthy for so great a banquet. The third unguent is the supereminent and superaffluent sweetness of God's priceless Heart, which not even the bitterness of death could lessen, and which is called the unguent of balsam. This unguent surpasseth every odour of spice, and is good for all languor of soul. Ask that this unguent may be poured out upon thy soul from the Heart of God, so that thou mayest taste and feel how sweet our Lord is, and having tasted His sweetness, mayest grow fat, and be enlarged, and comforted, and be made one body with Him, Who gave Himself to thee through such mighty love. And when thou feelest no sweetness from any of the things aforesaid, ask that this may be brought about in thy sweet Lover Himself, and that at least thy tastelessness may be tasteful to Him, and that all thy lukewarmness may glow in Him, and that He alone may be glorified in all thy works now and for the time to come."

Chapter X.

How man should recommend his faith to God.

IF any man shall recommend his faith to God in the following way, he shall obtain from God the grace never to be tempted at the end of his life as to the true faith. First, then, let a man recommend his faith to the Omnipotence of the Father, and pray to Him that he may be so confirmed by the power of the Godhead, as never to be able to fall away from the right faith. Secondly, let him commit it to the inscrutable Wisdom of the Son of God, and pray that he may be so lit up with the light of Divine knowledge, as never to be seduced by the spirit of error. Thirdly, let him recommend it to the benevolence of the Holy Ghost, with the supplication that his faith may so work, in Him, all things through love, as to merit to be found perfect and consummate at the hour of death.

Chapter XI.

Of the five sighs, with which man should go to sleep.

ONCE upon a time, she saw her own soul in the likeness of a leveret that seemed to sleep, but with its eyes open, in our Lord's bosom. And she said to our Lord: "O my Lord God, grant unto me that, like this little animal, when I sleep with my body I may watch before Thee in my mind." Our Lord answered her: "As the hare is said to ruminate and to sleep with its eyes (open), so ought man, when he goeth to sleep, to ruminate on this verse: 'Let my eyes take sleep, but my heart, let it watch before Thee; let Thy right Hand protect Thy servants who love Thee;' or let him meditate something about God, or speak with God, and thus, when he falleth asleep, his heart will watch before Me, and if any evil happen to that man in his sleep, if he feel anything troubling him, it is a good sign that he will never be separated from Me. Likewise, when man wisheth to sleep, let him draw a sigh, as it were, from My Divine Heart, in union with the praise which flowed forth from Me upon all the Saints, to supply for the praise with which every creature is bound to praise Me. Secondly, let him sigh again in union with that gratitude which the Saints draw from My Heart, and with which they give thanks to Me for the gifts bestowed upon them. Thirdly, let him sigh for his own sins, and the sins of all mankind, in union with that Passion by which I took away the sins of all. Fourthly, let him sigh in affection and desire of all the good which man stands in need of for the praise of God, and his own service, in union with that Divine desire of Mine, which I had on earth for man's salvation. Fifthly, let him sigh in union with all the prayer which poured forth from My Divine Heart upon all My Saints for the salvation of all, both living and dead, desiring that I should receive every breath which he breatheth that night, as if with a like intention he were to sigh before Me without ceasing. Then I, Who can refuse nothing to the prayers of a soul that loveth Me, will fulfil his desire in My Divine truth."

Chapter XII.

Of the Wedding-garment.

ONCE, when she heard the words read in the Gospel: "*Friend, why comest thou in hither, not having on a wedding-garment?*" she said to our Lord: "O my Beloved, what is the garment without which no man can come to Thy marriage?" Before long our Lord showed her a garment, marvellously wrought in purple, and white, and gold, and said: "This marriage-garment is made of the whiteness of a pure heart, and the purple of humility, and the gold of Divine love. Whosoever desireth to have this garment, must have his heart clean, so as not willingly to suffer any evil thought to cleave to his heart; and to determine and convert whatever he seeth or heareth, not to evil but to good. Moreover, let him subject himself in lowliness and sweetness of heart to those who are set over him, nay, to every creature for God's sake. Let him also love God with his whole soul, and count every creature vile in respect to God, nor so love anything at all, as to keep himself at a distance from God; nay, rather let him cast away such a thing altogether far from hin, and fly therefrom.

Chapter XIII.

In what the soul may be made like unto God.

WHEN the Mass was being sung: "*Dicit Dominus: Ego cogito cogitationes pacis et non afflictionis,*" our Lord said to her: "If thou wishest to be very dear and like unto Me, imitate Me in these words. For as I think the thoughts of peace and not of affliction, so do thou ever strive to have a quiet heart and peaceful thoughts, not contending with anyone, but patiently, humbly, sweetly conversing with all. So, also, as I hearken unto all who call upon Me, do thou show thyself easy of hearing, and of kindly will in all things; strive, moreover, to bring all out of their captivity, that is, to bestow help and comfort upon all who are in trouble and temptation."

Chapter XIV.

That God desireth our heart.

ANOTHER time our Lord said to her: " Seek Me in thy five senses, after the manner of a host, who looketh for the coming of a beloved friend before the door of his house, or who, by looking through the windows to see if he can perceive the guest whom he longeth for, remaineth always seeking for him. Even so let the faithful soul ever seek for Me in her five senses, which are the windows of the soul.

And if she behold what is fair and lovely, let her think how fair and lovely, and how good is He Who made them, and let her straightway stretch herself out towards Him Who made them. Moreover, when she heareth a sweet melody, or anything in which the ear taketh delight, let her think: 'Ah, how sweet will be the voice of Him Who calleth the happy souls, even the voice from which all sweetness and clearness of voice proceed.' Likewise, when she heareth men speak or read anything, let her always observe if she can hear anything in which she may be able to find her Beloved. In like manner, in all things that she saith, let her seek God's glory and her neighbour's salvation. Again, when she readeth or singeth, let her think: 'Ah! what is thy Beloved saying to thee, or commanding thee, in this verse or in that lection?' Let her seek Him thus in all things, until she perceive some sort of taste of the sweetness of God. In smell and in touch, in like manner, let her remember how sweet is God's Spirit, and how sweet will be His kisses and embraces. And in whatever creature she taketh delight, let her ever bear in mind the delights of God, Who hath created for us all things so fair and delightful and sweet, that He may allure and lead us to the knowledge and love of His own goodness. Wherefore let her resolve in her heart, that, if it were possible, she would most gladly pay to God all praise and thanksgiving, and every kind of service, which every creature is bound to offer Him. Likewise, let her be prepared to offer all the pain, tribulation, sorrow and labour, that ever a man hath borne for God's love." Once also, when she was praying for the portress, who was troubled by the guests who were coming in, she heard from God these words: "Every footstep which a man taketh out of obedience increaseth his reward, just as if, one by one, he were to heap up coins in My hand." Likewise our Lord said to her: "Man ought to receive what is necessary for the convenience of his body in union with the love with which I created all things for his use; secondly, in union with the love which I had on earth for My Father's honour and men's salvation; thirdly, let him accept labours and the service of those who minister to him in union with the love wherewith he himself is served for God's honour, that those who serve may be sanctified thereby."

Chapter XV.

What is the highest good that man can do?

ANOTHER time our Lord said to her: "The highest good and most useful thing that man can do with his mouth is to praise God, and frequently to converse with God, that is, to pray. So, too, the most praiseworthy thing before God, that a man can do with his eyes, is to shed tears of love, and continually to read the Holy Scripture. Moreover, for the ears, the best thing to do is gladly to listen to the Word of God, and to hold them bent down and ready to obey. And for the hands, the most fruitful thing to do, is to raise them in prayer, and to write holy and spiritual things. The most perfect thing also for the heart to do, is fervently to love and desire God with the whole heart, and to think of Him sweetly in meditation. For the whole body it is an exceeding useful exercise to make genuflections, and to keep vigils, and to perform works of charity. In like manner, let a man have other things in which he may take delight in God, namely, lowliness, charity, humiliation, thanksgiving; and in all things that happen to him, let a man say, 'Blessed be the Name of our Lord,' and 'Thanks be to God,' and at all times let him bless God.

Revelations of S. Mechtild,

VIRGIN,

Taken from the Fourth Book of her Spiritual Grace.

Chapter I.

How men may best advance in the religious life.

IT came to pass that, on a certain Friday, the pious and devout handmaid of God beheld our Lord Jesus standing at the Altar with outstretched hands, while His most holy Wounds, as if freshly inflicted, poured forth Blood in abundance, and our Lord said to her: "See how all My Wounds have broken out afresh to appease God the Father for you all." Moreover, the glorious Virgin Mary stood at the Right Hand of her Son, and she wore a crown of marvellous size, on which all her virtues and eminent graces, and all the mighty things which God hath worked through her, shone forth in a wonderful way. Then the Soul approached her, and besought her to pray for herself and the congregation. But she, with great reverence, kneeling down before her Son, devoutly saluted His Wounds, and commanded the Soul to act in like manner, saying: "Come thou also, and salute the Wounds of my sweet Son, which He hath borne in every member of His Body." And when she had gratefully done this, she prayed our Lord to reveal unto her what He wished them chiefly to observe, by means of which the religious life might be increased. He answered: "He who desireth to be a true religious, should guard his eyes from ever seeing, and his ears from ever hearing anything that may stain his heart. Let him also restrain his mouth from every useless word; and if he see or hear anything unprofitable, never let him suffer his mouth to speak thereon. Above all, let him guard his heart, lest at any time he should take delight in evil thoughts, or dwell upon them of his own accord. For a man cannot prevent such thoughts coming upon his heart, yet can he easily prevent himself consenting to them or willingly admitting them. Let him look, also, diligently into all his actions, and as often as he shall fall in any way, never let his heart rest, until he have asked pardon of his Lord, and let him resolve to confess his fault as soon as possible."

Chapter II.

What best preserves a man in the religious life.

ANOTHER time, as she was earnestly praying for her congregation, that God might keep them in His service for all time, and by increasing His grace in them make them to prosper in all virtue and good, she received the following answer from God: "As long as I find in them humble subjection, in humbly and simply obeying both those who are set over them, and one another; and in not only keeping, but also in loving, virginal chastity; and in giving thanks, together with sweet gratitude for all benefits, and in counting themselves unworthy of the same; and in preserving friendly love; and not only in loving God with a sincere heart, but also in loving one another in union with God, and in showing forth the works of charity; never will I turn away the eyes of My Fatherly protection from them, nor leave them in their hour of need."

Chapter III.

Of three things acceptable to God.

"IF a man wish to offer Me an acceptable gift, let him strive to exercise himself in these three things. First, let him endeavour to be faithful to his neighbour whenever he is in need or in trouble, and, as much as in him lies, to lessen and excuse all his defects and sins. And if he do this, then I will be faithful to him in all things of which he may stand in need, and I will cover his sins and negligences, and make excuse for him before My Father. Secondly, let him strive, in all his tribulation, to fly to Me alone, nor let him complain of his trouble to anyone, but to Me alone let him open up with confidence every grievance of his heart. Such a man will I never forsake in his necessities. Thirdly, let a man endeavour to walk with Me in truth, and then, at his last hour, even as a mother receiveth her loving child, will I receive him into My fatherly embrace, and he shall rejoice for evermore."

Chapter IV.

That those who are still alive are most happy.

ANOTHER time, when the community were communicating, and the handmaid of God was unable to approach on account of sickness, she asked our Lord to give her a few crumbs from His table. Before long it seemed to her as if our Lady, the most holy Virgin Mary, were sitting at a large table, together with all the Saints, and that she held out to her some crumbs, like unto little particles of gold and precious stones, communicating to her at the same time her own joy and beatitude. Then the Saints said unto her: "Ah! how happy are ye, who are yet alive upon the earth, and how much merit ye may gain; for if a man knew how much he could merit even in one day, his heart would be so enlarged with joy that such a day hath shone upon him, during which he may live to God, and by God's grace increase his merit to God's praise, that the whole of that day he would appear more prompt and strong in doing and suffering all that ought to be done or suffered."

Chapter V.

What man should do when he is in sadness.

AGAIN, as she was praying for a certain person who was in grief, she received this answer from God: "Let her often read this versicle: '*Blessed art thou, O Adonai, in the firmament of heaven, and glorious and for ever!*' And if at times it come into her mind to think that she is not among the number of the elect, let her do as a man would do were he in a dark valley; for if he saw the sun, he would gladly mount up out of the valley to the mountain tops, and escape the darkness; even so should he who is wrapped in the darkness of sadness, mount up to the mountain of hope, and look with the eyes of faith upon Me the true heavenly firmament, in which the souls of all the elect are fixed like the stars in the firmament of heaven. Wherefore it is a good thing for a man often to consider, with what free goodness I chose him, and how lovingly I thought of him, and changed all his evil for him into good. And let him bless Me in the eternal firmness of the elect, and say: 'Let all Thy Angels and Saints bless Thee together!' Moreover at this word: *'Let all Thy Angels and Saints bless Thee!'* let him desire that all the Angels and Saints should praise God together with him."

CHAPTER VI.

How man should commit all his grievances to God.

AGAIN, as she was praying for another person, she heard this answer come from God: "When man is burdened with trouble, let him prostrate himself at My feet, and there let him lay aside all his burden by committing it to Me, and say this prayer: *'Look down, O Lord, Holy Father, upon Thy servant, for whom our Lord Jesus Christ did not hesitate to be delivered into the hands of wicked men, and to undergo the torment of the Cross;'* and let him pray that I may look down upon him with the eyes of mercy, and give light into his soul, so that he may be able to recognize for what reason, and with how great love, I have permitted this to happen unto him, and thus patiently suffer this, as well as all adversity, to My praise. Then let him come to My Hands, and say this response: '*Send down, O Lord, Thy wisdom from the seat of Thy majesty, that it may be with me, and work with me, in order that I may know what is acceptable before Thee for all time;*' and let him pray that the Divine Wisdom may co-operate with him and help him, so that he may have strength to bear his heavy burden for God's glory, his own profit, and the benefit of all. Thirdly, let him come to My Heart, and say: '*O marvel encircling us round about, and admirable price of our redemption!*' and let him pray that by the love of My Heart, with which I bore the burdens of all men, I may cause him to bear the burden of his sadness with gratitude and love."

Chapter VII.

That whatever the Soul desireth should be sought in the Heart of God.

ONCE, having been asked by a certain person to pray to our Lord to give her a pure, humble, longing, and spiritual heart, she received and heard the following answer: "All that she desireth, and all that she standeth in need of, let her seek for in My Heart, and let her ask Me to give her, even as a child asketh of his father for all that he desireth. When she desireth purity, let her have recourse to My innocence. When she desireth humility, let her take it from My humility. Let her also supply her own desire from Mine, and smilingly take to herself My Love together with the whole of My Divine and religious conversation." Then she said: "My Lord, I ask of Thee that in her last moments Thou mayest act mercifully with her, and give her the certainty of remaining with Thee." To which our Lord made answer: "Who, that is wise, would throw away and lose the gold that he hath acquired with labour and cherisheth with love? All that is human in her I have sanctified by My Humanity, and all that is spiritual in her I have verified in My Spirit at her baptism, and now I will not forsake her any more for ever."

CHAPTER VIII.

How Christ supplieth the defects of a man out of His own fulness.

THE servant of God was once praying for a person who had complained to her of the sorrow of heart from which she was suffering, because she did not love God. Now the Saint herself had fallen into great sadness on account of this, thinking herself worthless, for never having loved God in all things, as He deserved to be loved, after all the great graces He had bestowed upon her. And our Lord said to her: " Ah ! My beloved, do not grieve, for all that I have is thine." To which she replied: " If, of a truth, all that Thou hast is mine, then, too, Thy love is mine. I offer Thee, therefore, this love, in order to supply thereby for all that is wanting in me." This our Lord graciously accepted, and said: " Thou hast done well, and whenever thou desirest to praise or love Me, and art not able to accomplish this according to thy desire, say to Me: 'O good Jesus, I praise Thee, and whatever is not in me I beg of Thee to supply for me.' Moreover, when it shall please thee to make acts of love, say to Me: 'O good Jesus, I love Thee, and whatever is not in me, I beg of Thee to offer to the Father in its stead the love of Thine own Heart.' And tell that person for whom thou prayest to act in the same way, and if a thousand times a day she repeat these words, and pray to Me in this way, so many times will I offer Myself for her to My Father, for I am not held back by any weariness or any disgust."

Chapter IX.

In what way man ought to have recourse to God.

ANOTHER time, as she was praying for a certain one, who desired to know what God chiefly desired of her, she heard the following answer: "Let her," He said, "hold herself in regard to Me, like the child who loveth to keep hold of his father, and always hath recourse to him when he wisheth him to give him anything, and whatever his father giveth for the affection with which he loveth him, holdeth it for something great and dear. So let her also pant after My grace, and never let her account as vain the things that I desire for her, but let her receive them with great gratitude, as having been given out of love, and give thanks for each of them. Secondly, let her behave like a royal spouse, who, neither for riches, nor for beauty, nor for noble birth, but for love alone is chosen, loved and promoted to the queenly glory. Such a spouse is naturally more faithful and ardent in her love; and if she have to suffer anything for the King's sake, will bear it with greater patience. Thus, also, she will always remember with gratitude, how freely I chose her before the foundation of the world, how I redeemed her with the price of My Blood, and called her, moreover, to enjoy My special love and friendship. Thirdly, let her behave like a friend with a friend, who thinketh all belonging to his friend above his own; and so let her seek God's glory in all things, and, as far as is possible, promote it, and whatever is opposed to God, let her nowise willingly suffer to be done. Moreover, in all these things, if at any time she obtain not anything that she may have desired, or if the grace which she hath sought after, or Divine consolation be taken away from her, let her not straightway be saddened, or think that this is done out of anger, or that she hath been forsaken of God: for a father who is true to his trust never giveth anything to his child that is not good for him; and at times the spouse treateth his bride like a servant, not out of indignation, but for her instruction. So doth God also wish to try the faithfulness of a soul, not that He Himself may know what she is, but that He may render her commendable before all His Saints.

Chapter X.

Of the three ways.

AS she was praying for a certain one in trouble, she received this answer from God: "I have walked in this world by three ways, and if any one desire to imitate Me, he must follow Me perfectly in these three ways. The first is dry and narrow; the second is full of flowers, and planted with fruit trees; the third is full of thorns and thistles. Now the first way is that of voluntary poverty, which I followed and loved in the highest degree all the days of My life. The second is that of My zealous and praiseworthy conversation: the third that of My hard and cruel Passion. Therefore must every one who desireth to follow Me embrace poverty, and desire to possess nothing in this world. Secondly, he must be praiseworthy in his behaviour. Thirdly, he must gladly suffer for My love both pains and tribulations.

CHAPTER XI.

That God is ready to receive those that are penitent.

ONCE when she was suffering from a severe headache, and as she was offering this pain to our Lord to His eternal praise, during Mass, at the oblation of the Host, together with the Host, immediately our Lord appeared to her, holding in His delicate hands a round piece of dry wood, which He seemed to be encircling with exceeding fair roses. And while she marvelled at this, she heard our Lord saying: "Understand by this, that never doth the heart of any sinner become so dry from the rust of sins,—if only he suffer some sorrow or infirmity of body, however small, with the intention that for My love and the praise of My Name he would gladly suffer greater sorrow or pain, if it were My will that He should do so,— as not to become, as it were, fresh and green again, and this too at that very moment, and by that very intention." Then she said: "If this is so, why is it, O most sweet God, that wretched man doth not feel this?" Our Lord said to her: "It is because he hath not as yet lost the taste for sin. For example, if a man after having done penance were so manfully to wrestle with his sins, as utterly to root out all taste for and delight in sin, beyond all doubt he would feel the sweetness of God's Spirit." Oh! the depth of Thy unsearchable Wisdom and Mercy, O most sweet God, Who endeavourest by such marvellous and many ways to draw the heart of the sinner to Thyself, that there is no longer any room for him to despair, since Thou followest after him with such graciousness, in order to recall him to Thy Fatherly arms.

Chapter XII.

A letter sent by Mechtild to a certain Matron.

O FAITHFUL soul, that lovest God, consider diligently and with burning love the law which the Imperial Child Jesus, the Son of His Father's Godhead and graciousness, gave unto thee when He chose thee for His bride, and bestowed Himself upon thee as a delightful Spouse, celebrating of Himself and by Himself those happy nuptials. On that day, then, of such solemnity, and of the joy of His Heart, He clothed Himself for the love of thee with a rose-coloured vestment, which love coloured for Him in the Blood of His own Heart. A garland of roses also He placed upon His Head, encircled with goodly pearls, even the precious drops of His own Blood. The gloves upon His Hands were so deeply pierced by love, that He could keep nothing in them, but poured out upon thee all that He had so long hidden in the world. His lordly couch was the hard Cross, on which He leapt with such joy and burning love, and with such delight, as never bridegroom took on couch of ivory and silk. On this couch of love He is still waiting for thee with desire unutterable. But if now thou desirest to be His bride, thou must utterly renounce all delight, and approach to Him on His little bed of sorrow, on which Love hath placed Him, and join thyself to His Side, which Love hath wounded. And consider diligently of what nature and how precious was the pledge He laid up for thee, when He opened for thee His Heart, even the treasury of His Godhead, and gave thee to drink therefrom in that goodly chalice, which healeth all the languor of thy soul. This is the exceeding goodly pledge of His priceless love, because it containeth all grace, all virtue, and all good. This pledge, I say, He will not take from thee, for thereby He hath confirmed His troth. Even as a king, who hath not as yet brought his bride into his house, leaveth a city or town full of wealth, and even his friends, as pledges that he will come and take her; so hath the Bridegroom thy Lover, given in pledge His most precious house, namely, His own Divine Heart, to God the Father, that He will never forsake thee, His own Bride, offering It at the same time daily for thee on the Altar, as a proof of the love with which He hath prevented thee from everlasting. Wherefore, O daughter of the Eternal Father, and elect bride of His Co-Eternal Son, and the Beloved and longed for resting-place of the Holy Ghost, love thy Beloved, Whose Heart is exceeding full of love for thee, and Who is Himself all love. Be faithful to Him, Who is faithfulness itself, and if aught troubleth thee, receive it as if it were a chain of gold which God hath put round about thee, whereby to draw thee to the love of His Son. Then straightway, as if consenting to be drawn in this way, lift thyself up, and also thine heart, that it may be still more drawn toward Him, and re-habilitated by grace and patience; observing diligently how by this God wisheth to work salvation in thy soul. Consider also, what may be wanting to thee in virtue. And if thou standest in need of humility, or any other virtue, lock up for thyself with the key of love the costly casket of all virtues, even the Divine Heart of Christ, and pray to the Lord of virtue, to give thee for aid His noble virtues, by which thou mayest overcome every temptation to sin. And if evil thoughts, those wretched robbers, rush upon thee, have recourse to thine armoury, and take therefrom the brightest of all arms, that is, the Passion and Death of thy Lord, and fix these as strongly as thou canst in thy heart by continual remembrance of them, that the whole crowd of evil thoughts may thereby be put to flight, and vanish away. Moreover, when any one despaireth of the goodness of God, which desireth that none should perish, but should come to the knowledge and love of the truth, except only those who desire of their own free will to be damned, let him remember that God is more ready to receive man than man is to come. And this above all doth God desire, that a man show himself ever in such a state, that He may be able to pour His grace upon him without ceasing, and ever increase in Him every good gift.

Chapter XIII.

A letter to a Matron, who was her spiritual daughter.

THE Lover of men, our Lord Jesus, desireth with a great desire, that the soul should be united to Him, especially that soul which desireth to be consoled by Him, and to experience His delights, and for this it is His Will that such a soul should cast away from her all consolation or delight in creatures, that doth not attract or move her to the love of God. For when a man hath anything that he loveth, or by which he is delighted, let him think with himself that God hath given him this, in order that thereby he may be moved to love Him. And if he feeleth that by this he maketh no progress in the love of God, but that that which he loveth cometh oftener into his heart than God, he ought to remove this love, whether it be for a man or any other creature, unless he desire to lose familiarity with God, for this familiarity with God is exceeding delicate, nor doth it suffer at all that anything be esteemed above it or even along with it, because the Son of the Father's Love desireth to be alone loved above all things, and to be the inmate of thy heart.

God hath given His Divine Heart to the soul, that she may give her own heart to Him in return. And if a man gratefully and trustingly do this, God's power will so restrain his heart that it will not be able to fall away into any great sin; that is to say, a man who hath a jealous love for the Heart of God, becometh more attentive in observing what is most pleasing unto God. And when he is sad, straightway let him fly with confidence to the treasure committed unto him, and there seek to be consoled. But if, the Wisdom of God so disposing, he is not consoled, nevertheless let him praise God, and give Him hearty thanks; for this is exceeding pleasing unto God in a faithful soul, who seeketh not her own, but the things which are Jesus Christ's, nor placeth her own consolation before God's honour.

Revelations of S. Mechtild,

VIRGIN,

Taken from the Fifth Book of her Spiritual Grace.

Chapter I.

Of the Charity of B. Mechtild to the dead.

THIS virgin, so remarkable for her piety and for her tender compassion for the afflicted, even as she always made commemoration of the living before our Lord, so also endeavoured by her devout prayers and suffrages to assist the Holy Souls. Hence it happened not unfrequently, when she prayed our Lord for the souls of the departed, which stood in no need of the help of prayer, that our tender and merciful Lord showed unto her their palms and their glory.

Chapter II.

Of a Sister who was sick.

A CERTAIN Sister, who had served God devoutly in holy religion all the days of her life, began to grow sick: and as the holy virgin was praying far more devoutly than usual, she saw her soul, as it were, kneeling before our Lord, and our Lord showing unto her His rosy Wounds, which she saluted in this versicle, which the servant of God had never heard before: " O health-giving Wounds of my beloved Lover, Jesus Christ, all hail ! all hail ! all hail ! in the Omnipotence of the Father Who hath given you, in the Wisdom of the Son Who hath suffered in you, in the graciousness of the Holy Ghost Who in you hath perfected the work of our redemption." Moreover, when she was obliged to receive the unction of the sacred oil, she saw two Angels who carried basins. By the water which was in the basins was signified Mercy and Truth, in which it was necessary for the soul to be washed from all stains, according to the words: "*Mercy and truth shall go before Thy Face.*" Then our Lord placed Himself near her by the side of the priest, and the Blessed Virgin Mary sat at her head. And when the priest read the Litanies our Lord signed her thrice with the sign of the Cross, and said: "I bless thee with sanctification and health both of soul and of body." And when the Blessed Virgin Mary was named, our Lady lifted up the sick sister, and said: "See, my Son, I give this Thy bride to Thee for Thine everlasting embraces." Each of the Saints also, as their names were invoked, bent their knees before our Lord, and prayed for her. And when the anointing was over, our Lord said to His Mother: "Behold! I commend her unto thee, that thou mayest present her spotless in My sight."

Chapter III.

Of the soul of an Infant.

A CERTAIN matron had resolved to consecrate her daughter to God before she was yet born, so that if the child should be a girl, she should be espoused to Christ. But within a year the little girl died, and her soul appeared unto the servant of God in the likeness of an exceeding fair virgin, clad in a rose-coloured vestment, over which was a mantle of cloth of gold, marvellously adorned with snow-white lilies; and she said to the girl: "Whence hath such great glory come unto thee?" She answered: "Our Lord in His graciousness hath bestowed it upon me. This red vesture signifieth that I was loving by nature; but the golden mantle representeth the habit of religion, which our Lord gave me because of my mother's vow, that I should lead the life of a religious." And as she marvelled at this, she received this answer from God: "Why marvellest thou? I have taken the integrity of her mother's will as if it had been accomplished, and have rewarded her for all the good things that she desired for her child, in this poor little girl." Then she asked of our Lord: "Why hast Thou taken away the maiden at so early an age?" He answered: "The little maiden was so lovely and loving that it was not expedient for her to live on earth. Moreover, her father would have taken no account of her mother's vow, and would have kept her in the world."

Chapter IV.

How, and with what intention, the Lord's Prayer should be said for the departed.

ONCE, upon a certain day, when she had communicated, she was praying to God and beseeching the most worthy Host for the liberation of the Holy Souls, that He Himself might be to them the forgiveness of all sins, and supply for all their negligences. And our Lord said to her: "Say for them one *Pater Noster* in union with the intention with which I gave that prayer from My Heart to be read by men." At these words she understood from God that she was to say the prayer with the following intention : At the words *Pater Noster qui es in cœlis*, she was to desire that indulgence might be given to the Holy Souls, for not having loved with sufficient reverence, nor duly honoured so worshipful and loving a Father, Who out of mere compassion had raised them to the dignity of being called the sons of God, and, moreover, for having angered Him so many times by their sins, and for having very often cast Him out of their hearts, in which it was His will that He should dwell and reign as in His own heaven ; praying at the same time in union with the loving penance and satisfaction which our innocent Brother Jesus Christ performed for them, that He would receive the love of our Lord's Heart with the same reverence and honour which He showed

Him during His human life, in atonement for these sins. *Sanctificetur nomen tuum:* These words she was taught to offer in satisfaction for their having never worthily venerated the Name of God their Father, and for often having even taken it in vain, and for having but seldom thought with attention on this Name, and also for having made themselves unworthy by their bad living of that most worthy Name, by which Christians are called after their Master Christ; desiring that He would deign to receive that perfect holiness of His Son, whereby He extolled His Father's blessed Name by His preaching, and honoured it in all the works of His Humanity. At the words: *Adveniat regnum tuum,* she was to have the intention of desiring that indulgence might be given to the Holy Souls for never having fervently desired, nor diligently sought after the kingdom of God, nay, even after God Himself, in Whom alone is true rest and joy everlasting; and, at the same time, to pray that He would receive the most holy desire of His own loving Son, whereby He wished them to be sharers and joint-heirs with Him in His kingdom, in satisfaction for all the sloth with which they had practised good. *Fiat voluntas tua:* at these words she was to desire that indulgence might be given them for not having preferred God's will before their own will, nor loved it in all things; and also to pray that God would receive the union of His Son's sweet Heart, and His prompt obedience, by which He was obedient even unto death, as amends for all their disobedience. At the words: *Fiat voluntas tua,* she understood in a special manner that those are guilty of great sin who seldom offer their will fully to God, and who, moreover, when they have offered it, oftentimes take it back again, and that it is very necessary that at these words special mention should be made of them, because by this negligence they are kept at a very great distance from God. *Panem nostrum quotidianum da nobis hodie:* at these words she was taught to desire that indulgence might be given them for not having received that most noble and to them most useful Sacrament, with sufficient longing, and for many of them having made themselves unworthy of it, and for very many of them rarely or never having received it at all; and she was taught to pray, at the same time, to God the Father, to receive that most fervent love, and ceaseless desire, and great holiness and devotion of Christ His Son, whereby He bestowed upon us this gift that surpasseth all gifts. At the words: *Et dimitte nobis debita nostra*, she was taught to desire that all their sins might be forgiven them, which they had committed in the seven criminal vices, and in those which proceed from them, and for not having forgiven those who sinned against themselves, and for not having loved their enemies; and also to pray to God to receive His Son's charitable prayer that He prayed for His enemies. *Et ne nos inducas in tentationem:* at these words she understood that she was to desire that indulgence might be given them for not having resisted their vices and lusts, but for having so many times consented to their enemy and the flesh, entangling themselves of their own free will in many evils; and she was taught to pray, at the same time, to the most Holy Trinity, to deign to receive all the labours and sufferings of Christ in satisfaction for all the past negligence of the souls in purgatory, and to free them from all evils, and to bring them to the kingdom of glory, which is God Himself. Amen.

After she had said this prayer with the above intention, she saw a vast multitude of souls giving thanks to God with exceeding great joy for their liberation.

Chapter V.

That we can be purged from venial sins by works of charity, but our mortal sins must be blotted out by the Sacrament of Penance.

ONCE, when this person had called and accounted herself unworthy of these gifts, two of her familiar friends, desiring to satisfy for her in this matter, resolved to pay to God for her, by means of the antiphon, "From Whom are all things, by Whom are all things, in Whom are all things, to Him be glory for ever," as many songs of praise as she had lived days upon the earth. And as she herself offered these praises to God in union with the love with which all gifts had flowed forth from His Heart, she saw a great river of exceeding purity flowing impetuously from the Heart of God, and cleansing from every stain the souls of those who had prayed for her out of charity. And our

Lord said: "Thus do all the works of charity purify a man from every venial sin; but mortal sin, because it cleaveth strongly to the soul like pitch, must be rubbed off by confession and greater contrition. Moreover, I keep all the works of charity in My Heart, as a treasure especially dear to Me, until he who has performed them come to Me, and then I give them back to him for the increase of his reward and glory."

Nor were these prayers sufficient for one of her friends, who loved her exceedingly in Christ, but, desiring to satisfy for her negligence to the highest degree, higher than which she could not satisfy, she caused to be celebrated for her, by the religious brethren and devout priests, as many Masses as there had been years of her life, and the Mass chosen was that which begins with the words: *Benedicta sit Sancta Trinitas*, in praise of the Most High and Worshipful Trinity.

Chapter VI.

How we ought to pray for those who are captive in body or in soul.

AGAIN, our Lord said to her: "He who desireth to pray with profit for those who are in captivity of body or of soul, let him pray to Me by the love which kept Me captive for nine months in the Virgin's womb; secondly, by the love which bound Me in swaddling-clothes and bands; thirdly, by the love which gave Me over bound into the hands of My enemies; fourthly, by the chains in which the Jews delivered Me bound into the hands of the judge; fifthly, by the chains whereby I was fastened to the column for My scourging; sixthly, by the nails with which I was fixed to the Cross; seventhly, by the binding in which, when I was dead, I was wrapped in the Winding-sheet, and enclosed in the Sepulchre, that by this love those who are in any kind of chains or sins may be loosed from them all."

Chapter VII.

How God commended this His handmaid to His own Mother.

ONCE, as she was reading the Gospel *Stabat juxta crucem*, she said to our Lord in the affection of her soul: "Commend me, O Lord, to Thy Mother, even as Thou didst commend Thy beloved John to her, and her to John." Straightway our Lord heard her prayer, and gave her into His Mother's hands, and said: "I commend to thee, O Mother, this soul, that even as thou wouldst desire to care for and soothe My Wounds and Myself, were I lying wounded before thee, so thou mayest cherish her with care, and console her in all her pains. I commend her also to thee, that thou mayest remember at how great a price I have valued her, since for the love of her I refused not to give Myself over unto death. I commend her also to thee, as that in which I have placed all the delight of My Heart, for My delights are to be with the children of men." Then the soul said: "O Lord, wilt Thou do this to all who desire it of Thee?" He answered: "Even so, for with Me there is no acceptance of persons."

Chapter VIII.

Of the praiseworthy conversation of Blessed Mechtild.

THINKING the above revelations sufficient, although, indeed, we might add many things, it is not our desire to proceed further with them, lest, being over-long and over-many, they should become tedious to those who read them, which God forbid.

We have also passed over so many things, that these that have been written are few in respect to those which we have omitted. Moreover, we have set these things forward for the glory of God alone, and for the profit of our neighbour, and also because we thought it would be an unworthy thing to hide in silence so much that is useful, not only to ourselves, but also to those who are to come hereafter. As, however, we have not described the praiseworthy and truly marvellous life and conversation of this venerable woman, we would wish, at least, before we end, to say a few words in commendation thereof, so as to leave an example to those who wish to imitate her behaviour.

This venerable woman, then, preserved her virginity, which from her seventh year she had vowed to God, and her purity of heart, with such great diligence that from her infancy she was without any sin. This is testified by her two confessors, who tell us, that never had they seen any man or woman with a heart so large or so pure as this woman, and her sister the Lady Abbess.* Wherefore, when she had made a general confession, the only little sin she could remember ever having committed—and this she confessed with great sorrow—was having once said, when she was a little girl, that she had seen a thief in the court, when she had not seen one; yet no

* S. Gertrude.

other falsehood did she remember to have knowingly and of her own free will committed. Not unworthily, then, may she be compared with the virgins who follow the Lamb, for she herself hath most perfectly followed the Lamb whithersoever He goeth. For neither was humility wanting to her, to lift her to the lofty heights of His glory; nor virginal chastity, to unite her to Him in familiarity and sweetness.

She may, also, without inconsistency, be likened to the fathers of the religious life, since, for Christ's love, she despised the world with its flowers, and embraced poverty to such a degree, that she refused to have even what was necessary. Even when compelled by obedience she had only one goodly robe; the rest were but of poor and cheap cloth, while the tunics which she wore were much torn, and mended in every place, and all this, when she might have had in sufficiency whatever she wished. On the other hand, all belonging to religion she had in perfection; that is to say, denial of her own will, self-humiliation, promptitude of obedience, earnestness in prayer and devotion, abundance of tears, enjoyment of careful contemplation. So far had she denied herself, and, forgetful of herself, had become absorbed in Christ, that she made but little use of her outward senses; hence it often came to pass that, without knowing it, she eat what was putrid, until it was discovered by those who sat near her and marvelled at her. In like manner, at times, without knowing it, she eat meat, until returning to herself at the laughter of the others, she found out what she had done. She poured forth doctrine in such abundance, that never hath there arisen one like unto her in our convent, nor, alas! we fear, will there ever arise. Everywhere the sisters gathered around her, as if about to hear a preacher of the Word of God. She was the refuge of all and the consoler of all; and by a singular gift she had this grace, that men opened to her with confidence the secrets of their own hearts. And many who have been delivered by her from their grievances, not only within the cloister, but also outside, and religious men and those living in the world were wont to say, that never had they received so much consolation from any man as from this woman. She dictated and taught so many prayers, that if they were all written together they would exceed the psalter in size.

She was so continually troubled with pains and infirmities, that not undeservedly she may be accounted to have had fellowship with the Martyrs. Moreover, she afflicted herself with many chastisements for sinners, and once upon a time, before Lent, when she heard the people singing lascivious songs, she was inflamed with exceeding great zeal for God, and loving compassion; and in order to make, at least, some amends to God, she placed in her bed broken bits of glass and other sharp fragments, and throwing herself upon them, rolled about for so long a time that her skin contracted and became one large bleeding wound, from which the blood poured forth in such abundance, that for pain she could neither sit nor lie. She had so marvellous a devotion to the Passion of Christ, that she could hardly hear it spoken of without tears, and very often when men were speaking of Christ's Passion without love, she was inflamed with such fervour, that her face and hands appeared in colour like unto a crab that hath been cooked. For this reason we believe that she frequently shed her blood spiritually for the love of Christ. This devout disciple of Christ was also united to God in such familiar converse, and had so offered all her will to God, that as she herself related, after she had made her profession, she never in anything had any other will than that which it was God's will should be done. She fed with marvellous sweetness on the words of the Gospel, and was moved to such tenderness, that very often, as she was reading it in choir, she passed into so great a state of jubilee, that she could not finish: at times she became, as it were, half dead; and so fervently was she ever wont to read it, as to excite to devotion all who heard her. In like manner, when she sang in choir, she fixed her thoughts upon God with her whole strength, as if she were all on fire; now stretching out her hands, now lifting them up on high; at other times, carried away, as it were, in ecstasy, she remained unconscious when others drew her along and moved her; or, at least, with difficulty, returned to herself.

And now, what more shall we say? May she not be likened to the angelic spirits? Yes, even with these she was joined so lovingly and in such friendly harmony, as seldom to be without their presence. Moreover, the comparison with the Angels, whose proper office it is to minister, agrees well with her, who, by her dutiful charity and sweet company, ministered compassionate love to the wretched, the help of prayer to sinners, admonition and correction to the negligent, the word of instruction to the ignorant. Of the sick she took exceeding great care, so that never was she so much occupied as to neglect visiting them every day, and asking them anxiously whether they had need of anything, being ever ready to minister unto them with her own hands, either to amuse them, or to make their beds. And when she grew old and infirm, even then she caused herself to be carried to the sick, and at times, not being able to speak, she still showed them, by gestures and movements of her head, such loving compassion as to move many to tears. Frequently she took part in all the lowest kinds of work, and especially in the common labours along with the sisters; sometimes she was the first of all to labour, at other times she worked alone, until she induced those who were subject to her, or rather attracted them by her example and kind words to help her. Like the archangels she interceded with many before God, and tenderly besought help for them from Him. She may be compared also with the Virtues, for she was an exceeding bright exemplar of all virtues. Nor undeservedly may she be counted amongst the Powers, since the Almighty Majesty gave Itself so often into her power, and she herself had been made so powerful over the demons, as they themselves once complained in a vision to a certain other person, saying, that by her merits and intercession the souls of the faithful were daily taken out of their power. With the Principalities, also, she may rightly claim a place, for like a princely commander, together with her sister the Venerable Lady Abbess, she wisely and orderly governed both the inner and outer life of the monastery. Moreover, not inconsistently is she joined with the Dominations, since she hath been proved to have been the sovereign mistress of her affections and acts. She was mistress over her heart, by keeping it in all custody. She was mistress over her works, by performing them for God's sake. She may also be called the most delightful Throne of God, on account of the exceeding fervour and purity of her mind; for, full of the grace of God, she pointed out what they ought to do to all who asked of her, how they should live and govern themselves, as if from the mouth of God Who dwelt within her. She may be likened, also, to the Cherubim, for, plunged so many times into the very source of Wisdom, and penetrating into the abyss of light, she illuminated with knowledge and doctrine all who came to her, like the sun shining in the temple of God. For as she herself told us, our Lord gave her often spiritual understanding as to the psalms, and whatever she either sang or read, and she understood what before had not entered into her thoughts. In like manner, most suitably and worthily this angelic virgin may be compared with the Seraphim, for so many times was she immediately united to Love itself, which is God, and so lovingly pressed to His burning Heart, that she was made one fiery spirit with Him. So gracious was she in speaking of God; so fervently, above all, did she discourse of charity, as often to inflame the hearts of those who listened to her. Wherefore it may be fitly said of her, that her words were as the words of Elias, which burnt like torches. In charity and devotion to God she was most fervent; in tenderness and anxiety with regard to her neighbour exceeding high; in humility and self-affliction the first of all. She was of a most tranquil mind, and kept her heart so free from, and unoccupied by cares in the time of prayer, that very often, when called from prayer to the grill, or to other business, straightway, as soon as she returned, she found again the same purity of prayer as she had left before she had been obstructed from prayer. In sickness she was so gentle and kind, and so cheerful and patient in everything, that she made all who came and ministered to her merry and joyful. Nay, never did her illness grow so strong as to prevent her becoming more cheerful, just as if she suffered nothing, when she heard men speaking of, or even uttering one word about God. Never was she found idle; for she was always either working what was useful with her hands, or praying, or teaching, or reading.

These few words in praise of her conversation we have written down.

"*O quam pulchra est casta generatio cum charitate!*"

PUBLISHED BY RICHARDSON AND SONS,
26, PATERNOSTER ROW, LONDON; AND DERBY.

Mediæval Library of Mystical and Ascetical Works.

The Mystical and Ascetical works of the Middle Ages, so remarkable for beauty, simplicity, wisdom and holy unction, with a few exceptions, are to most English-speaking Catholics, almost unknown. The difficulty of obtaining them, and the language in which many of them are written, have hitherto stood in the way of their being read and studied.

It has been thought, therefore, that by a careful selection and translation of the more important of these works, much good might be done to souls, while at the same time, our Blessed Lord would be still more glorified in His Saints and Servants. With this object in view, and by the advice of those whose opinions are of greater value than his own, it is the intention of the translator of the "Book of the Visions and Instructions of B. Angela of Foligno," to issue a "Mediæval Library of Mystical and Ascetical Works."

Under this title will be published such works as :—

The Meditations of S. Anselm.

The Marian Writings of S. Bernard, with the Sermons of Abbot Guerric.

Selections from the Works of Hugh & Richard of S. Victor.

The Golden Little Book on Cleaving unto God, by B. Albert the Great.

Selections from the Works of S. Thomas of Aquino.

Selections from the Writings of Tauler.

Revelations of Mother Juliana, Anchorete of Norwich. (In the Press.)

And many other useful and valuable works.

ALREADY PUBLISHED.
Price Six Shillings, superfine cloth, Post 8vo.
MEDITATIONS ON THE

Life and Passion of our Lord Jesus Christ.

BY DR. JOHN TAULER, DOMINICAN FRIAR.
Translated from the Latin by a Secular Priest.

Price 3s.

The Fiery Soliloquy with God,
OF THE REV. MASTER GERLAC PETERSEN,
Throwing light upon the solid ways of the whole Spiritual Life.
Translated from the Latin by a Secular Priest.

PUBLISHED BY RICHARDSON AND SONS,
26, PATERNOSTER ROW, LONDON; AND DERBY.

Price 4s.

The Book of the Visions and Instructions of B. Angela of Foligno,

As taken down from her own Lips
BY BROTHER ARNOLD of the Friars Minor.
Now first translated into English by a Secular Priest of the Third Order of S. Dominic.

This Day, small 8vo. superfine cloth, price 4s.

SPIRITUAL CONSOLATION,
OR A TREATISE ON THE PEACE OF THE SOUL,
From the French of Pere Lomber,
Interspersed with various Instructions necessary for promoting the practice of Solid Piety,

BY THE AUTHORESS OF "THE URSULINE MANUAL."

NOW READY, Superfine Cloth, price 2s.

MEDITATIONS ON
The Way of the Cross.
BY L'ABBE H. PERREYVE.
Edited in English
BY A PRIEST OF THE DIOCESE OF BIRMINGHAM.

NOW READY, price 4s. 6d.

Spiritual Letters of
FATHER SURIN, S.J.
FIRST SERIES.
TRANSLATED BY SISTER M. CHRISTOPHER,
Order of S. Francis.
WITH A PREFACE BY FATHER FRANCIS GOLDIE, S.J.
EDITED BY THE REV. H. COLLINS.

These most beautiful Letters, addressed to Religious, and to devout people living in the world, are a golden treasury of maxims and instructions for the spiritual life.

NOW READY, price 5s.

The Christian Trumpet;
OR, PREVISIONS AND PREDICTIONS
About impending General Calamities, the Universal Triumph of the Church, the Coming of Antichrist, the Last Judgment, and the End of the World.
COMPILED FROM THE WRITINGS OF THE SAINTS and eminent Servants of God, and other approved Ancient and Modern sources,
BY A MISSIONARY PRIEST,
With Superior's permission.

www.ingramcontent.com/pod-product-compliance
Lightning Source LLC
Chambersburg PA
CBHW020806230426
43666CB00007B/884